THOMAS MARENT
with Ben Morgan

rainforest

Jackson's chameleon
(*Chameleo jacksoni*), Mount
Kenya National Park, Kenya.

Blush butterfly (*Cithaerias menander*), Braulio Carillo National Park, Costa Rica.

Weevil (Circulionidae), Tambopata Reserve, Peru.

Golden lion tamarin
(*Leontopithecus rosalia*), Poço
das Antas Reserve, Brazil.

Orb web spider (Araneidae),
Tangoko Nature Reserve,
Sulawesi, Indonesia.

Panther chameleon
(*Furcifer pardalis*),
Andasibe, Madagascar.

Nymphalid butterfly (*Callicore eunomia incarnata*), Rurrenabaque, Bolivia.

Passionflower (*Passiflora sanguinolenta*), Ecuador.

Juvenile or male Wagler's pitviper (*Tropidolaemus wagleri*) with female, Borneo.

Dragonfly (Odonata),
Relais de Patawa,
French Guiana.

Treefrog (*Boophis*),
Mantadia National Park,
Madagascar.

Toadstool (*Leucocoprinus birnbaumii*), Tambopata Reserve, Peru.

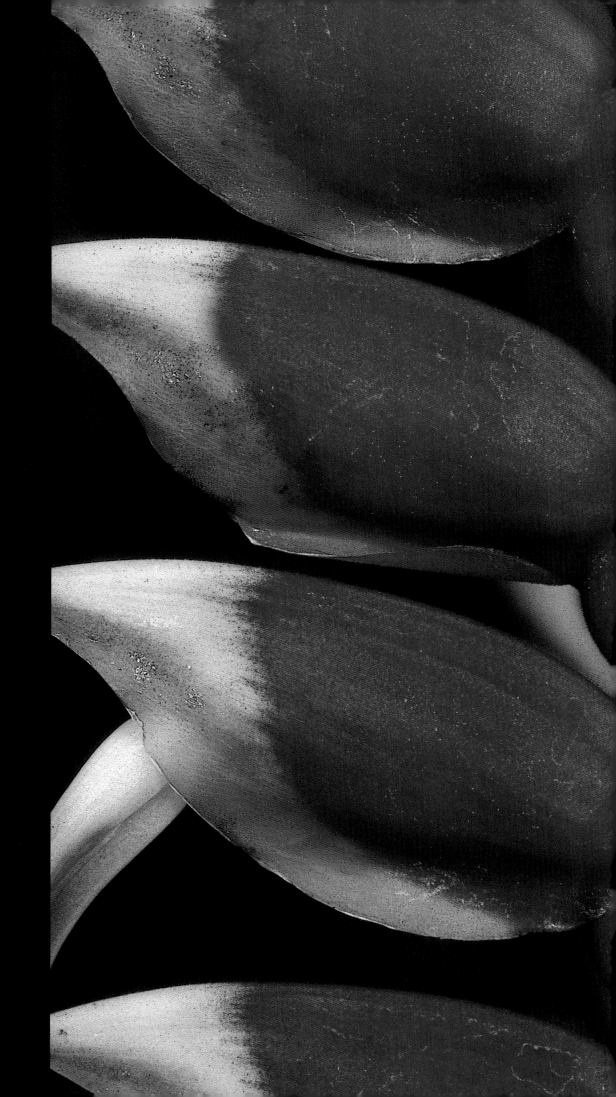

LONDON, NEW YORK, MELBOURNE,
MUNICH, AND DELHI

PROJECT ART EDITOR Victoria Clark
DESIGNER Timothy Lane

EDITORS Ed Wilson, Giles Sparrow

CONSULTANTS Dr Kim Dennnis-Bryan,
Derek Harvey, Dr George C. McGavin,
Dr Mark O'Shea, Dr Simon Loader

MANAGING EDITOR Debra Wolter
ART DIRECTOR Bryn Walls
PUBLISHER Jonathan Metcalf

DTP DESIGNER John Goldsmid

PRODUCTION CONTROLLER Heather Hughes

INDEXER Jane Parker

First published in Great Britain in 2006
by Dorling Kindersley Limited
80 Strand, London WC2R 0RL

A Penguin Company

A CIP catalogue record for this book
is available from the British Library

ISBN-13: 978-1-4053-1530-2
ISBN-10: 1-4053-1530-X

Colour reproduction by Media Development
Printing Ltd in the UK
Printed and bound by LEO Paper
Products Ltd in China

Printed on acid-free paper derived from certified
sustainable European forests, produced in an ISO 14001
and EMAS certified mill. No wood from rainforest
areas was used in the manufacture of this book.

See our complete catalogue at
www.dk.com

contents

foreword

Today, tropical rainforests cover just six per cent of the Earth's land surface, yet they are believed to contain at least half of all the species on the planet. Some scientists believe that there could be millions of species in the largest swathes of rainforest – in South America's Amazon Basin, Africa's Congo Basin and in Southeast Asia. Many of these plants, insects and animals are yet to be scientifically studied, and others have not even been named. In fact, because most rainforest wildlife is found high up in the inaccessible tree canopy, many thousands of species are probably yet to be identified.

Extraordinary new discoveries are being made all the time. In 2006, deep in the rainforest-clad mountains of the island of New Guinea in Southeast Asia, an expedition found an area untouched by humans – a "lost world" – and with it a new bird, several species of frog, some butterflies and plants, all previously unknown to science.

Some may ask, "why should we bother to try and protect obscure rainforest animals and plants that few of us will ever have the chance to see?" But the fact is that, over the last few hundred years, the wealth of resources found in rainforests has proven to be of enormous benefit to the survival and well-being of humankind. From foods and beverages such as bananas, avocados and cocoa, to medicines such as quinine (and many others for treating a wide range of diseases, including cancer) and industrial products derived from the Brazilian rubber tree, the biological diversity of rainforests has had a profound effect on the development of human society. Many of the rainforest's secrets have been revealed to us by indigenous peoples, whose livelihoods and cultures depend on their environment and who often have a deep knowledge of wildlife.

This collection of Thomas Marent's images, which has been 16 years in the making, brings alive the sheer and awe-inspiring beauty of many of the rainforest's plants and creatures. We can but wonder at the diversity, the complexity and the uniqueness of what nature, over time, has produced. This book is not only an astonishing photographic achievement; it also provides a powerful and compelling reminder that, whatever their potential value to humankind, rainforests should be protected as precious and irreplaceable, in their own right. The Earth, and humanity, would surely be the poorer without them.

Simon Counsell
Director, The Rainforest Foundation UK

a photographer's passion

I first set foot in a rainforest in 1990, when I was 24 years old. I was in Australia studying English, which I'd missed at school in Switzerland. When the course finished, I did what lots of young travellers do in Australia: I bought a second-hand car and hit the road in search of adventure.

I had always loved nature. I grew up in Switzerland, which is home to some of the most spectacular scenery on Earth. When I was 16 I bought my first camera, and from then wildlife photography became a lifelong hobby. So in Australia, I was naturally drawn to the lush and exotic forests of the tropical northeast, which seemed a million miles away from the alpine meadows and pine forests of Switzerland. It was the rainy season and the forest was bursting with life. It was hot, humid, noisy, and completely exhilarating, but most exciting of all was the wildlife. Exploring with a camera was like being on a treasure hunt. I found insects and animals of every hue and shape. I was immediately hooked.

There and then, I made up my mind to explore rainforests throughout the world, starting with the great forests of Latin America, which became my favourite destination. I returned year after year, discovering new things on each visit. For me, one of the great joys of wildlife photography is this sense of discovery. Studio photography involves minute planning – you start out with a preconceived mental image and try to create it. But in nature the thrill of the unexpected adds an extra dimension. You might see nothing for days and suddenly stumble across a tiny, bug-eyed spider that has never been photographed before. Then the challenge becomes an aesthetic one: how can you best capture the animal's character, the intricate detail of its body, an impression of its habitat, the atmosphere of natural light – all before it disappears back into the undergrowth?

On the first few trips I relied on serendipity alone, photographing anything beautiful that I saw. Gradually, however, I became much more

ambitious and began to seek out particular subjects. So I visited Sulawesi to photograph spectral tarsiers, Costa Rica for quetzals and tent-making bats, and Uganda for chimpanzees. But even with the help of expert guides, my trips often failed. I had to visit Borneo twice to photograph the enormous *Rafflesia* flower, and it took three trips in Peru to capture the cock-of-the-rock.

Rainforest animals don't normally reveal themselves willingly. The majority are shy, elusive, or nocturnal, but this adds to both the challenge of finding them and the thrill of capturing them on film. It would be dishonest of me not to admit that an element of danger also adds to the excitement. Tropical forests are difficult and dangerous places – the terrain is treacherous, the weather is often terrible, and rivers can rise by metres overnight and wash away your camp. There are a multitude of venomous insects and snakes, many of them deadly. Even more disturbing and unpredictable are confrontations with people – in Colombia I narrowly escaped being found by guerillas with a reputation for kidnapping westerners. But the

greatest danger is also the most mundane: getting lost. It happened to me on numerous occasions and was terrifying every time. The most memorable was a trip through the coastal jungle of Colombia, where my guide and I were disorientated for more than a day. I thought I would die from heatstroke or starvation, but fortunately the sound of the sea led us to safety.

Yet none of the dangers or discomforts of working in the rainforests seem to matter when you capture a rare or beautiful creature on film. To me, the rainforests are the greatest treasure houses of natural riches on Earth, and I think it is tragic that we are losing them just as we are beginning to appreciate their true value. We not only have the power to destroy these beautiful and important habitats, we also have the power and the responsibility to protect and preserve them.

> " I bought my first camera at the age of sixteen. I have been passionate about wildlife photography ever since. "

Thomas Marent

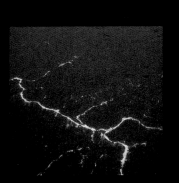

panorama

> **"** Every rainforest is different, yet all have the power to overwhelm your senses with life's sheer intensity and raw beauty. **"**
>
> THOMAS MARENT

"A great wild, untidy, luxuriant hothouse" was Charles Darwin's first impression of the tropical rainforests of Brazil, penned during his round-the-world voyage on HMS *Beagle* in the 1830s. Awed by the majestic evergreen trees tangled with massive lianas, by the kaleidoscope of exotic butterflies and birds, and by the incessant drone of insect life – audible from the ship anchored offshore – Darwin struggled to find words that could do justice to his excitement and delight. But his reaction was unusual for the times in which he lived. To most of Darwin's contemporaries, the rainforest was a fearful place to be avoided at all costs. Explorers and writers portrayed it as a dark and threatening jungle, a land of dense, impenetrable vegetation, treacherous swamps, poisonous animals, and hostile natives.

By the 20th century, conservationists were describing rainforests as the world's greatest biological treasures, the "lungs of the Earth", an ecosystem as fragile as a house of cards, and one on which all life depends. So what are rainforests really like? For most visitors, the first impression is not of kaleidoscopic colours or oppressive darkness but of a world that's shady, damp, and unremittingly green. Animals,

at least at first glance, seem surprisingly scarce, apart from the occasional squawk or flutter of wings high in the treetops overhead. The air is heavy with moisture, warm, and still. The sky is as likely to be overcast as blue, though it hardly matters since little of it can be seen from the shade of the forest floor. Far from being an impenetrable jungle, the forest floor is often spacious, open, and easy to walk through. Trees rise like giant columns, their bark smooth and trunks branchless nearly all the way up to the canopy. The biggest are propped up by stabilizing roots that flare out of the base and snake across the ground. Others appear to be supported by stilts. Here and there are breaks in the tree cover that let hot sunshine reach the forest floor, allowing palms and saplings to prosper. And everywhere there are climbing plants: lianas hanging like tangled ropes and knotting the treetops together; vines creeping up the trunks and over shrubs; orchids, ferns, and mosses sprouting from the branches.

This is lowland tropical rainforest — "true" rainforest, and the jungle of popular perception. It doesn't matter whether the location is South America, Central Africa, or Southeast Asia, lowland tropical rainforest looks, smells, and sounds more or less the same all over the planet. The spreading treetops form its upper tier — the sun-drenched canopy, a lumpy, uneven affair made up of trees of widely varying heights. Occasional giants, known as emergents, tower high above the rest of the canopy, their crowns exposed to the full force of the weather. Beneath the canopy is a less distinct layer — the understorey, a varied assortment of palms, vines, shrubs, and saplings awaiting their turn in the canopy. And beneath the understorey is the forest floor, a jumble of dead leaves, occasional seedlings, fallen boughs, and knobbly roots writhing across the thin soil.

Lowland tropical rainforests form a ragged belt around Earth's equator, straddling major continents and dotting islands across tropical seas.

They flourish only where the weather is wet and warm all year round. They are not the hottest places on Earth – the temperature is normally between 24°C and 28°C, well short of the high 40°C or 50°C that occur in deserts. However, tropical rainforests experience no marked cold season. In fact, the temperature varies more between night and day than over the whole year.

Equally important is the consistent length of a day. Because of the Earth's tilt, temperate countries enjoy long sunny days in summer when they're tilted towards the Sun but they experience shorter, darker days in winter when they're tilted away. At the equator, Earth's tilt hardly matters, and there are around 12 hours of daylight and 12 hours of darkness on every day of the year. This means plants have no distinct growing season and can photosynthesize all year round.

Water is the lifeblood of a rainforest. A true rainforest needs at least 1,700 mm of rain a year (though some places receive eight times as much),

and this rain must be spread across the year. Consistently heavy rain each month is perfect, but in practice it never happens. Despite the myth that seasons don't occur in rainforests, all experience some seasonality in their rainfall. In true rainforests such as those of the Congo River Basin in Central Africa and the Amazon rainforest in South America, there isn't exactly a dry season – just a wet season and an even wetter one, when the forest is liable to flood. Water is abundant all year round, and plants are able to grow without interruption. As a result, the trees that grow there are mostly evergreen, though some do periodically shed their leaves as part of the rhythmic cycles of flowering and growth.

As you travel away from the equator, rainfall becomes increasingly seasonal and the character of the forest changes. Rainforests merge into "semi-evergreen forests" or "monsoon forests", which have a distinct dry season when some of the trees shed their leaves, and tend to be less diverse

> # " Virgin rainforest can feel like a lost world, a reminder of what our planet was like before nature was tamed by humanity. "
>
> THOMAS MARENT

than tropical rainforests. In turn, these merge into "tropical dry forests", where the dry season is longer and the majority of trees shed their leaves. In the wet season, these types of forests can seem almost as lush as a rainforest, though there are fewer of the dangling lianas and climbers that give true rainforests their riotous appearance.

Where rainforests meet mountains, another type of ecosystem prevails. "Cloud forests" are swathed in cool mists that form as humid air rises from the lowlands and chills. The trees are shorter than in a rainforest but are smothered in greater numbers of "epiphytes" – plants that take root on

branches and absorb their moisture from the damp air. So rich is the profusion of plant life that cloud forests can seem more lush than rainforests.

The world's most famous rainforests are found in the tropics, but there are also temperate forests that arguably deserve the same label. The rich, evergreen forests of southwest New Zealand and North America's Pacific coast appear as green as tropical forests, and are covered with epiphytes to rival the wettest of cloud forests. But the most vibrant, complex, and diverse rainforests in the world – those that inspired Charles Darwin – are to be found in the heart of the tropics.

panorama

◁◁ A river snakes through the lowland rainforest of Colombia's Pacific coast. Annual rainfall in sections of this forest can exceed 13 m, making it the wettest rainforest on Earth.

The upper layer of lowland tropical rainforest – which is known as the canopy – is the greatest realm of life on Earth, home to perhaps 40 per cent of all the species on the planet, many of them unseen and unknown. Trees provide living space for the canopy's residents. In their fight for light, they battle for position, some growing head and shoulders above the rest and casting neighbours into shade. Nearly all are decked with lianas, vines, and epiphytes – plants that sprout in the treetops. The canopy basks in light but faces the brunt of the weather, battered by rain one minute and parched by the sun the next.

◁▽ Seen from a hill on the northeast edge of the Amazon rainforest, the canopy stretches to the horizon, a sea of green dotted with yellow where trees are in flower.

◁ Sunbeams pierce the canopy at Lamington National Park, a subtropical rainforest in Queensland, northern Australia.

While the canopy is drenched with sunlight and rocked by storms, the world below is dark and still. On the forest floor, the air is heavy with moisture and rings with the drone of cicadas. Animals and plants are shielded from wind and scorching sunlight, but the gloom presents another challenge. Plants need light to survive, yet as little as 1 per cent of the direct sunlight falling on the canopy reaches the forest floor. Clearings where trees have fallen enable light to filter through, but most of the seeds that sprout down here are doomed.

△ Palms flourish around a rainforest creek in northeastern Australia. Creeks provide precious patches of light on the gloomy forest floor.

△ Mossman Gorge National Park, Australia

△ Amacayacu National Park, Colombia

Dominating the forest floor are the winners in the battle for light. Giant trees, called emergents, tower over the canopy and need enormous "buttress roots" to stabilize them against the wind. Buttress roots have evolved in different species throughout the world's rainforests, some forming triangular fins, others twisted into elaborate, sinuous shapes. As they divide and snake their way into the ground, they stay close to the surface, their microscopic tips probing the thin soil for nutrients leaching out of leaves, dung, and corpses.

▷ Buttress roots provide both support and sustenance to the biggest trees in a rainforest. Tangkoko Nature Reserve, Sulawesi.

For plants that start life on the gloomy forest floor, sunlight is in short supply. One solution to this predicament is to cheat. Climbing plants coil their way round the trunks and branches of other plants, taking a shortcut to the sunny treetops and dispensing with the need to invest in trunks of their own. Some climbers cling to trunks using roots like suckers and inch their way up, the trailing end withering as new growth develops at the top. Others drape themselves over saplings and wait to be hoisted up as their hosts mature into trees. Their stems and roots mature into woody lianas that hang from the canopy like ropes and weave the trees together, creating aerial walkways for animals.

◁ A liana corkscrews around a tree on its journey up to the canopy in Manú National Park, Peru.

△ Lianas are pulled and twisted into elaborate loops and tangles as the trees that carry them grow. Manú National Park, Peru.

△ Strangler figs grow downwards, enveloping their host in a lattice of aerial roots that graft together. Manú National Park, Peru.

△ The twists and turns of mature lianas are full of grooves and crevices that become hiding places for animals. Tambopata Reserve, Peru.

A creeper snakes along a dead
branch in its search for sunlight.
Gorgona Island, Colombia.

In the foothills of the Andes, in South America, where the land rises, lowland rainforest gives way to cloud forest. It may look as lush and steamy as rainforest, but cloud forest is much cooler, its climate tempered by altitude and a veil of mist that screens the sun. Stunted by the chilly air and foggy light, the trees are much shorter than in lowland rainforest, the canopy is lower and the forest floor brighter. The air is so damp that plants can take water directly from it and don't need roots in the ground. Mosses, ferns, lichens, and orchids grow as epiphytes on every branch, smothering the trees in dripping vegetation and giving cloud forests an eerie atmosphere.

◁ Clouds of mist melt into the undulating canopy of a cloud forest at El Reventador, Ecuador.

Verdant mosses and vines hang like beards over a creek in a Colombian cloud forest.

Fed by mountain glaciers, freshwater streams tumble through the cloud forest of Venezuela's Sierra Nevada National Park.

> " Where rainforests meet mountains, you can find fascinating ecosystems like the cloud forests of the Andes or the huge tepuis of Venezuela. I'd long dreamed of photographing the tepuis from the air, but it wasn't easy. Helicopters were expensive so I hired a Cessna aircraft and removed the doors. By the time we arrived, the mountains had vanished under a sea of cloud and we had to turn back. The same happened the next day, and the day after that. Finally, on day four, the view was clear. It was freezing in the doorless cockpit, but the views were fabulous and I was speechless with wonder. For a closer look at this mysterious 'lost world', I climbed to the top of Tepui Roraima, an arduous 8-day trek. "

◁ Tepui Chimanta, a sandstone table-mountain in the Chimanta Massif, rises abruptly from the rainforest of southern Venezuela.

△ A carnivorous pitcher plant (*Heliamphora*) flowers on Tepui Roraima. Most of the plants on the tepuis' summits are found nowhere else.

▷ Tree ferns give New Zealand's Fiordland National Park an exotic feel. They thrive in shade but their "trunks", which consist not of wood but a mass of fibrous roots surrounded by the bases of dead fronds, grow only a fraction a year.

△ The monstrous roots of this tree were partially wrenched from the ground as the tree fell. Fiordland National Park, New Zealand.

About 5,000 km south of the equator is a forest that bears a striking resemblance to those of the tropics. The temperate rainforest of New Zealand's South Island flourishes in the country's rain-soaked southwest corner, within deep valleys gouged out of the land by ice-age glaciers. Winters here are mild, and moisture-laden winds from the Tasman Sea bring heavy rain all year round, creating ideal conditions for evergreen trees such as the silver beech and native conifers. In the damp air, mosses and vines grow with uninhibited luxuriance, forming a vast dripping green carpet over everything, and tree ferns dominate the understorey, their elegant crowns echoing the palm trees of the tropics.

Tangled tree ferns vie for space on the forest floor of Fiordland National Park, New Zealand.

◁ With up to 7.6 m of rain per year, New Zealand's Fiordland National Park is awash with streams and rivers. The land is so wet and steep that this part of the country has never been inhabited by humans.

△ Mosses cover every spare surface in Fiordland National Park, from fallen logs to riverside boulders.

Dew glistens on a blade of grass.
Rainforests absorb water and
release it back into the air,
forming clouds and more rain.
Machu Picchu, Peru.

Water is the lifeblood of the rainforest. Much of the rainfall is soaked up by plants, but the rest succumbs to the force of gravity. Creeks fill within minutes after a downpour and become treacherous to cross, often being as deep as they are wide. Their gurgling waters tumble white over rocks and collect in deep, clear plunge pools, where the underlying sand and impurities in the water can create intense colours.

Clockwise from top far left: Venezuela, Uganda, Malaysia, Australia, Venezuela, Peru.

Rainforest hills are riddled with babbling streams, like this one in Kinabalu National Park, Borneo. The moist rocks provide a perfect habitat for mosses, of which Kinabalu has at least 300 species.

△ ▷ Monsoon forest surrounds opalescent pools and waterfalls at Erawan National Park, Thailand.

"Although tropical forests are often much more dark and oppressive than people imagine, some places do seem like the clichéd garden of Eden – especially when a long, hot trek leads to pools of tranquil water that are perfect for swimming in. At Erawan National Park I hiked up the 'seven-tiered waterfall' – a 2-km stretch of river with seven separate waterfalls, all of them like a scene from paradise. The river bed here is a cream-coloured limestone that somehow intensifies the water's natural hue to create mesmerising shades of blue and jade, like the colours you see in coral lagoons. The pools were just the right temperature for a swim, though fish tend to nibble your toes. Erawan is not true rainforest but semi-evergreen, its seasons governed by the monsoon. In the dry season the trees look dusty and streams dwindle, but in the wet season the area is as lush as any jungle."

▽▷ At Jasper Creek in Canaima National Park, Venezuela, the river tumbles over tiers of red jasper, a semi-precious mineral.

" Jasper Creek is a magical place, a unique waterfall where the action of flowing water has polished the bedrock over hundreds of years to form glistening sheets of jasper. Local Indians call it Kako Paru, meaning 'fire creek', because of the rock's fiery golden-red glow. You need a lot of luck to photograph this natural wonder. The river bed is usually hidden under deep water, so you need a dry spell first to bring down the water levels. Then the light has to be perfect. Bright sunlight creates too much contrast, but under an overcast sky the light is heavy and colours are muted. I was lucky. After several rainless days, the water dropped and the light was just right. I could wade out onto the falls to take close-ups of the rock, which had a metallic brilliance where the water sluiced over it. "

"" You can feel Iguaçu Falls rumbling in your feet before you see it. Next you hear its thunder and feel the mist on your face. Finally you step to the edge of a gaping chasm and the ground drops away, revealing the most spectacular waterfall in South America. This is where Brazil's mighty Iguaçu River, having gathered strength for more than 1,000 km, plunges over the edge of a gigantic, shattered slab of basalt rock – the remains of a prehistoric lava flow. Every second, 5,000 tons of water hurtles down into a mist-filled abyss, producing clouds of spray and rainbows everywhere. It's easy to see why some people call it 'Niagara on Viagra'. ""

◁ Iguaçu Falls lies on the border of Brazil and Argentina, where the Iguaçu River pours off a basalt plateau in 275 separate cascades.

▽ The most violent part of Iguaçu Falls is "the Devil's Throat" – a horseshoe formation where 14 waterfalls join in the wet season to form a deafening wall of water.

As the water from highland streams enters the lowlands, it creates new habitats that add to the complexity of the rainforest. Slow-flowing rivers meander across the land in sinuous loops that can get cut off to form oxbow lakes and swamps. The rivers are not just a source of water and fertile silt but a source of light, as they carve vast gashes through the canopy that let sunlight reach plants all the way down to ground level. As a result, rivers are often bordered by a mass of tangled vines and trees that creates the impression of an impenetrable jungle, even though the forest beyond may have a cavernous, open understorey.

▷ A fallen tree clings to life on the edge of the Sarapiqui River, Costa Rica. River banks are dynamic habitats, disturbed by cycles of flood and erosion.

▽ Sluggish waters like this creek in Manú Park, Peru, provide hiding places for caimans. In the rainy season, the Manú River bursts its banks, and submerges much of the forest, allowing fish and river dolphins to swim among the trees.

On their winding journey to
the sea, lowland rivers merge
and grow, pooling an ever-greater
load of sediment. In the Amazon,
there are two varieties of lowland
river: whitewater and blackwater.
Whitewater rivers, laden with
sediment, are the colour of
cappuccino. The water may look
filthy but it's teeming with life
and is home to the rare Amazon
river dolphin, which uses sound
rather than vision to hunt in
the murk. In stark contrast,
blackwater rivers carry no
sediment and are almost lifeless.
Their waters look unnaturally
clear, with the reddish-brown
tint of black tea. Such rivers are
poisoned by tannins — chemicals
that plants manufacture to defend
themselves. The tannins from
rotting vegetation seep into the
water, making the rivers acidic.

◁ Blackwater and whitewater
rivers merge and mix in Canaima
National Park, Venezuela.

Fallen flowers from a sea poison tree (*Barringtonia asiatica*) rest on the black volcanic sand of a beach in Tangkoko Reserve, Sulawesi.

▷▷ The sun sets over the Pacific coast rainforest in Chocó, Colombia.

diversity

> ## There are so many different species in a rainforest that you can walk for an hour without seeing the same species twice.
>
> THOMAS MARENT

Night falls swiftly in the rainforest, filling the shady understorey with an inky, impenetrable blackness. Out of the gloom comes a sound — the metallic "tink tink" of a treefrog calling for a mate. Another joins him, this one coarser, more grating. Then another, different again, a trilling that sounds almost electronic. Soon there are dozens, hundreds, a thousand different voices that rise and fall in reverberating crescendos, seeming to emerge from the air itself.

The nocturnal chorus of frogs embodies not just the exuberance of life in tropical rainforests but also its diversity. A rainforest is a hothouse of evolution, a place where plants and animals have diversified into myriad different forms in the endless struggle to survive. Species adapt, split, and change, spawning innumerable variations, branches on an evolutionary tree that never stops growing. So great is the degree of diversity that rainforests harbour more than half the world's plant and animal species, yet they cover a mere six per cent of the land surface of the Earth.

The statistics defy belief. While Europe has only 53 native frog species, the rainforests of Peru and Ecuador have more than 300. On a wet night you might hear 80 calling within the same area of

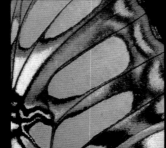
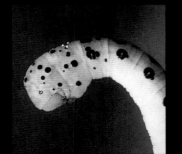

forest. Sharp eyes and a flashlight reveal their appearances to be as diverse as their songs. Some, barely the size of your fingernail, are covered in lurid red blotches. Others are brilliant green with white bellies, glossy black with yellow stripes, the colour of mud or the shape of a leaf. Even more diverse are the insects. A single tree in a rainforest may be home to more than 40 species of ants, and one species of tree may harbour more than 150 beetle species that live nowhere else. Trees, too, reach astonishing levels of diversity. One hectare of rainforest can contain as many as 250 different species — more than ten times the number found in a hectare of temperate forest.

How rainforests can sustain such a wealth of species is an enigma. The equatorial climate must be a factor, since diversity is known to decline towards the poles. Another factor may be the forest's physical structure, its lushness, largeness, and complexity creating many more niches, both physical and ecological, than exist elsewhere.

Then again, the origins of diversity may be biological. Perhaps competition for resources causes species to diverge, each carving out an increasingly specialized niche that minimizes overlap with competitors. Parasites and predators may also be a factor. If a species becomes common it risks being overwhelmed by these enemies, and so evolution favours the rare. And if most species are rare, there is room for many.

It was once thought rainforests owed their diversity to antiquity and an equable climate — an endless summer that has endured for millions of years. But now it appears that the opposite is true. During the ice ages, rainforests dried out and fragmented repeatedly, each time forming islands where new species may have arisen in isolation. Even today, rainforests are endlessly disturbed by storms, tree falls, and floods. Perhaps this continual turmoil keeps life in flux, preventing the strong from dominating and, consequently, allowing thousands of species to coexist.

diversity

◁ This noctuid moth caterpillar (*Rhanidophora*) from Kenya's coastal forests is one of 165,000 known species of butterflies and moths – most of them tropical – that make up the order Lepidoptera. Butterflies reach their peak diversity in the rainforests of Peru, which are home to an estimated 4,000 native species.

◁◁ Frogs, like this Gunther's banded treefrog (*Hyla fasciata*) in Tambopata Reserve, Peru, are amazingly diverse in rainforests. In parts of Peru, more than 80 species live within sight and sound of each other – as many as live in the whole of the United States.

" After a long period of rain, fragile little fungi sprang up everywhere in Peru's Manú National Park, even on tiny twigs and the middle of dead leaves. The endless variety of shapes and colours was enchanting. Some were like delicate little flowers borne on impossibly thin stalks. Others reminded me of coral formations. They were fresh for only an hour or two and then quickly began to shrivel up, vanishing as quickly as they'd appeared. "

◁ Mushrooms (*Favolaschia*) proliferate on a rotting log after heavy rain in Manú National Park, Peru.

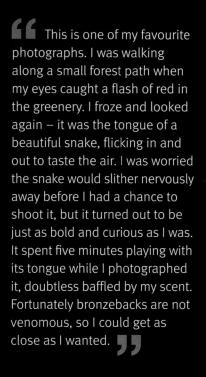

◁ A painted bronzeback snake (*Denderelaphis formosus*) tastes scents in the air at Kinabatangan Wildlife Sanctuary, Borneo.

▷ Venezuela in South America is home to some 21,000 plant species, including this flowering plant (Melastomataceae) found in the country's Sierra Nevada National Park. Rainforests are thought to harbour at least 40 per cent of the world's 300,000 plant species, including two-thirds of all known flowering plants.

◁◁ A female Borneo orang-utan (*Pongo pygmaeus*) in Sepilok Forest Reserve, Borneo.

❝ I was just about to leave the orang-utan sanctuary in Borneo's Sepilok Forest Reserve when I spotted this female orang lying on the ground. There was something remarkably human in her sad expression as she toyed with the leaves in front of her. It struck me as odd that she was lying on the ground rather than idling in a tree, as orang-utans prefer to do, but then I realized why: she only had one arm and presumably wasn't able to climb. Sepilok Rehabilitation Centre is one of the world's oldest orang-utan sanctuaries. On the edge of a protected area of virgin rainforest, it helps young orang-utans that have been rescued from captivity to adjust to life in the wild. ❞

▷ This ruffed lemur (*Varecia variegata*) is one of the unique animals found on Madagascar, the world's fourth largest island. More than 70 per cent of Madagascar's species are endemic (found nowhere else), a result of the island's long isolation from the rest of the world's landmasses.

◁◁ Katydids are part of the grasshopper family and come in a bewildering array of shapes and colours. This female, shot in Sumatra in Indonesia, is one of 6,000 katydid species worldwide, the majority of which live in tropical rainforests.

◁ Claws at the ready, this spiny crayfish (*Euastacus sulcatus*) prepares to defend itself from attack in northern Australia's Lamington National Park.

◁◁ Harvestmen (Opiliones) are harmless relatives of spiders that feed on detritus on the forest floor and so help to recycle dead material. Of the estimated 5,000 known species in the order Opiliones, the vast majority inhabit the tropical rainforests of Latin America and Southeast Asia.

◁ The saucer-shaped caps of these Colombian cup fungi (*Cookeina tricholoma*) capture raindrops, which help dislodge and disperse their spores. Fungi are as diverse in lifestyle as in appearance. Some live entirely on dead matter, others parasitize the living, and still others live symbiotically with plants, helping their roots to extract nutrients from the soil.

◁◁ Australia's Peppermint Stick Insect (*Megacrania batesii*) is so-called because it exudes a peppermint-scented liquid. It lives exclusively on *Pandanus* plants in the northeast of the country. This degree of specialization enables thousands of diverse species to co-exist in the rainforest.

▷ This beautifully camouflaged orchid mantis (*Hymenopus coronatus*) from Borneo waits motionless in an orchid flower, ready to ambush pollinating insects. Both orchids and mantids are at their most diverse and numerous in tropical rainforests. Orchids make up what is possibly the largest family of flowering plants (Orchidaceae), with at least 24,000 species and perhaps as many as 30,000.

◁◁ A weevil (*Eupholus bennetii*) displays its blue and black coat, Crater Mountain, Papua New Guinea. Weevils are the biggest beetle family, with at least 48,000 known species, and doubtless many more still to be discovered.

◁ This red cracker (*Hamadryas amphinome*) is one of at least 1,200 butterfly species found in Tambopata Reserve in Peru. In Europe, there are just 400 species.

◁◁ A common chimpanzee (*Pan troglodytes*) peers through the undergrowth at Kibale National Park in Uganda. Kibale has the greatest concentration of primates on Earth, with 1,000 chimpanzees and perhaps a dozen species of monkeys and bushbabies.

" In Uganda my guide and I tracked chimps for four days. My guide gave me strict orders to keep at least 8 metres away from the animals, but I made the mistake of getting too close. One of the chimps, alarmed by my presence, started screaming, shaking branches, and thumping the ground. Then the whole group followed. I was petrified. Chimps are fantastically strong, and they can be brutally violent. My guide whispered that I should keep totally still and avoid eye contact. I stared at the ground and waited, my heart pounding so hard I could feel it in my throat. After a minute, the chimps began to quieten, and I started edging away. "

▷ The swivelling eyes of this
chameleon (*Furcifer*) from the
island of Madagascar can focus
on two places at once, giving it
an advantage in stalking prey.
Chameleons are found throughout
Africa, but they reach their greatest
diversity in Madagascar, which
is home to half of the world's 134
species. The island's chameleons
range in size from the pygmy
stump-tailed chameleon, which is
barely longer than a thumbnail, to
the cat-sized Parson's chameleon,
the world's largest species.

◁◁ The extraordinary diversity of
rainforest birds is partly explained
by the year-round abundance of
insects and fruit. Birds such as
the toco toucan (*Ramphastos toco*)
are predominantly fruit eaters –
an ecological niche that does not
exist among temperate birds.

{-}

◁ The red mouthparts stand out conspicuously on this otherwise well-camouflaged katydid (Tettigoniidae) – one of some 2,000 katydid species native to the Amazon rainforest. Virolin National Park, Colombia.

◁◁ Spiders are more diverse in rainforests than elsewhere and the constant warmth allows them to live longer and grow bigger than their temperate relatives. The largest spiders are the tarantulas, of which there are some 850 species, nearly all found in the tropics. This tarantula is rearing up in a threat posture, displaying its fangs. Tambopata Reserve, Peru.

"I went to Madagascar's Andasibe National Park in search of the golden mantella frog. It was raining and there were frogs everywhere, but although I could hear the 'tink tink' calls of the golden mantella, the sounds were difficult to pinpoint on the forest floor. But then I stumbled across this beauty – a *Boophis* treefrog. Treefrogs are much smaller than photographs of them suggest. This example was only a couple of centimetres long, with feet so translucent I could see through them."

◁ This treefrog (*Boophis viridis*) is one of at least 50 different species in the Madagascan genus *Boophis*. Some are so similar they can only be identified by their calls.

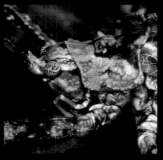

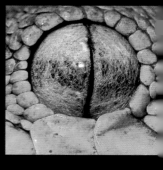

survival

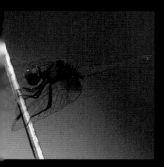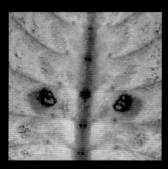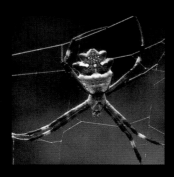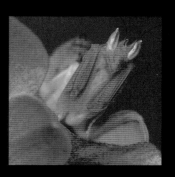

> " It doesn't take long to realize that a rainforest is a battleground – sooner or later, every organism becomes a target for attack by something else. "
>
> THOMAS MARENT

A rainforest may appear to be a natural paradise, but it is one with a paradox at its heart. This great abundance of life, and this much diversity, come about through an unparalleled struggle for survival. For plants, much of the struggle happens in slow motion, played out over years as they compete for a share of life-giving sunlight. If months were seconds, trees would shoot upwards and push their neighbours aside for territory; vines would writhe around trees and suffocate them; and smaller plants would multiply along branches as they extend, infesting trees like parasites and weighing them down until they eventually collapse. Winning a space in the sun is far from the end of the battle. Sunlight is just a means to an end for a plant – the energy it needs to manufacture nutrients out of air and water through the process of photosynthesis. The next challenge is to hold on to those nutrients in the face of attempts to steal them. Rainforest plants come under continual attack from animals that want to chew their leaves, suck their sap, bore

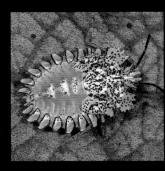

though their wood, and gnaw into their seeds. Spines and thorns may deter some animals, but most of the plants employ less conspicuous defences. A great many use chemical weapons, lacing their leaves with indigestible, foul-tasting or poisonous compounds. Others employ armies of soldiers – pugnacious ants that hurry to the plant's defence should anything touch it.

Plants have the ability to synthesize food but animals have to acquire it. To survive, they must feed on other organisms, and to succeed in doing so they must get round their chosen victims' defences. For herbivores in a rainforest, this means overcoming chemical defences. Many animals have evolved an immunity to specific poisons and in doing so have become specialized to feed only on the plants that produce them. Other animals are generalists – they feed on a wide range of plants but must search for gaps in the plants' armoury, seeking out fruits, nectar, or tender young leaves and buds, all of which tend to be poorly defended.

Predators largely avoid the issue by eating animals instead of plants, but this brings problems too. While plants are rooted to the spot and easy to catch, animals can hide, run away, or fight back. Predators, therefore, need acute senses to locate their victims, speed and strength to capture them, and specialist equipment to immobilize them.

Predator and prey are locked in an evolutionary battle that never ends. As predators evolve more cunning and deadly means to ensnare their prey, so prey evolve more ingenious means to elude and repel their predators. Many rainforest animals have become masters of disguise, their bodies so effectively camouflaged that they are impossible to see until they give themselves away by moving. Animals that don't hide often use an opposite strategy, displaying lurid colours to warn of poisons in their bodies. But not everything is what it seems. Rainforests are full of fakes – animals using mimicry to appear more poisonous, bigger, or more fierce than they really are.

survival

predator

Hunting is a challenge when prey have a thousand hiding places, so rainforest predators need stealth and patience to capture their victims.

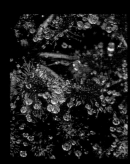
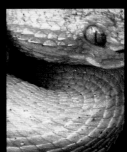
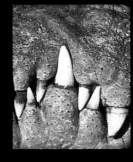

There are great benefits to be had from eating flesh rather than plants. Animal tissue is not only packed with calories but also functions as a metabolic filter, concentrating beneficial nutrients and eliminating the foul toxins that make so many rainforest plants inedible (though animals may use defensive poisons too). There is, however, a disadvantage to the predatory way of life: animals are much more difficult to ensnare than plants. Predators need cunning, sharp senses,

lightning reactions, and weapons that are specialized. Strategy is also crucial. Prey are able to flee and conceal themselves in the dense vegetation of rainforests, so strategies based on stealth and surprise yield better results than those based on pursuit. Many predators turn the thick cover to their advantage, stalking prey furtively until they are close enough to strike. Others employ a "sit and wait" strategy. Lying motionless and silent, they wait patiently for unwary prey to

△ Slit-like pupils enhance the 3D vision of this green vine snake (*Ahaetulla prasina*) from Borneo. ▷ Mantises are ambush predators. Their spiky front legs can flick out and trap prey.

come toward them. Because of the need for stealth, most rainforest predators hunt alone, but not all are solitary: on the forest floor, predatory ants rove in armies of up to 20 million, overwhelming prey, such as spiders, lizards, and frogs, through sheer force of numbers.

" It wasn't until I looked through the telephoto lens that I saw what was in the toucan's mouth – a baby bird, plucked from its nest. This may seem like repugnant behaviour in a fruit-eater, but in fact toucans are part-time carnivores. Fruit contains little but sugar and water, so toucans also eat insects, lizards, eggs, small birds, even snakes. Nestlings are easy pickings. The distressed parents are so intimidated by the toucan's monstrous bill as it looms towards the nest that they daren't attack until the bird flies away. Unfortunately, by then it's too late. "

◁ Small animals, such as this nestling, supplement the largely fruit-based diet of the keel-billed toucan (*Ramphastos sulfuratus*). Sarapiqui River, Costa Rica.

Even the most well-hidden animal will eventually give itself away by moving, so the best way to spot prey is often to lie still and watch. This is the strategy deployed by a praying mantis. Camouflaged to blend in with the vegetation, it waits motionless until prey move into snatching distance. Its enormous compound eyes see the slightest movement and have overlapping fields of view, enabling the mantis to judge distance before striking. Once caught, victims are consumed immediately.

▽▷ One mantis (top) falls prey to another (bottom and right). Mantises (Mantidae) attack the necks of their victims, often decapitating them. Harau Canyon Reserve, Sumatra, Indonesia.

Tarantulas are nocturnal hunters. Instead of trapping prey in webs, they lurk in dark crevices and ambush passing animals. They attack with amazing speed and will tackle anything small enough to overpower – even small bats. Though equipped with eight eyes, they rely on touch rather than vision to hunt. Special hairs on their legs detect the vibrations of moving prey with such sensitivity that the tarantula can pinpoint its location and size. The victim is dispatched with an injection of paralysing venom from two large, sickle-shaped fangs. The venom also liquefies the animal's internal organs, as spiders can only consume liquid food.

▷ A purple tree spider (*Tapinauchenius purpureus*) rears up in a defence posture, revealing a pair of blue fangs. Camp Caiman, French Guiana.

> **"** Some people run screaming at the sight of a tarantula, but to me these creatures are objects of beauty. They might look grubby and hairy at first glance, but if you look closer you often see splashes of colour, such as red knees, pink toes, or cobalt-blue legs. An even closer look through a macro lens reveals that even their hairs can be beautiful. The menacing appearance of tarantulas belies their true nature. They never attack people without provocation, and many are so docile they can be kept as pets. **"**

◁ A Colombian lesser black spider (*Xenesthis immanis*) tiptoes around fungi growing on a fallen tree at Tambopata Reserve, Peru.

△ A Peruvian tarantula straddles a banana leaf. Tarantulas that hide in banana plants sometimes find themselves shipped abroad. Manú National Park, Peru.

△ The metallic pink toe (*Avicularia metallica*) starts life with a pink body and dark-coloured feet and undergoes a reversal in colouration in adulthood. Fourgassier Falls, French Guiana.

△ Tarantula hairs act as sense organs, waterproofing, and a barrier to parasites. Many species also possess "urticating hairs", which sting like nettles. Tambopata Reserve, Peru.

While tarantulas use touch to hunt by night, jumping spiders use sight to hunt by day. They have the sharpest vision in the spider world, with bulbous eyes that can resolve detail, colour, and depth. Once a jumping spider has spotted its prey, it stalks like a cat, creeping stealthily closer. Then it pounces, launched into the air by a hydraulic mechanism in the rear legs. Vision is important in the sex lives of jumping spiders, and some species perform courtship dances that rival those of birds of paradise.

▽▷ Many tropical jumping spiders (Salticidae) are vividly coloured with iridescent hairs arranged in patches and spots. The spider at right is from Lae, Papua New Guinea.

△ Pantanal, Brazil.

△ Pantanal, Brazil.

△ Manú National Park, Peru.

△ Amacayacu National Park, Colombia.

△ Chocó, Colombia.

△ Chocó, Colombia.

Whip-spiders (Phrynidae), impale prey in a cage of spikes and pull the victim to their eviscerating jaws. Corcovado National Park, Costa Rica.

Jumping spiders are not the only hunters with outsized eyes. Tarsiers' eyes are bigger than their brains and are the largest eyes, relative to body size, of any mammal. Curiously, tarsiers are nocturnal but their eyes lack the reflective "tapetum" that helps other mammals see in the dark. The eyes are too large to move in their sockets, but tarsiers can look round by swivelling their necks like owls. Despite the cute appearance they are fierce predators, leaping on everything from birds to venomous snakes.

▽▷ The spectral tarsier (*Tarsius spectrum*) posesses such quick reflexes it can snatch insects from the air. Tangkoko Nature Reserve, Sulawesi, Indonesia.

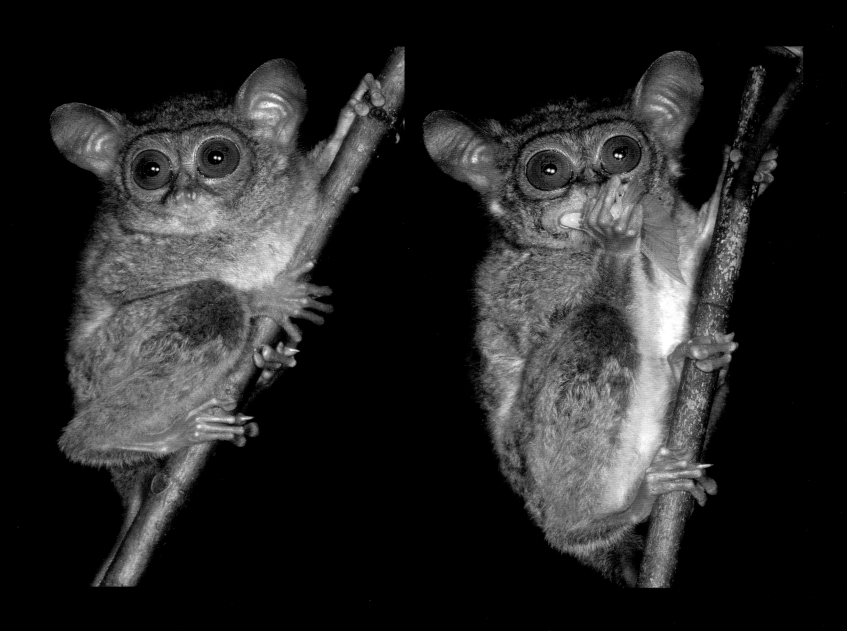

The black caiman (*Melanosuchus niger*) – the largest predator in the Amazon – is supremely adapted to aquatic life, with eyes and nostrils at the top of the head. This partly submerged male waits for prey, its eyes a magnet for mosquitoes.

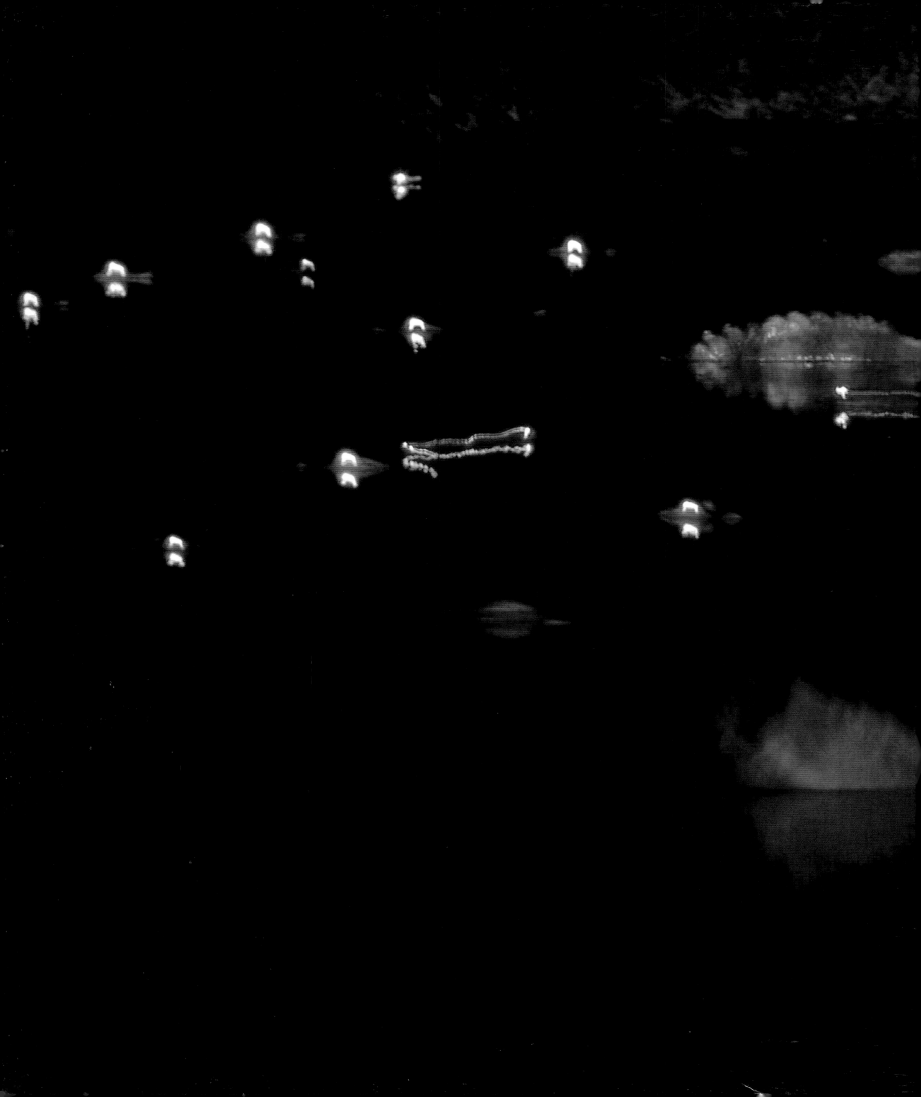

Night is a great time to look for caiman because that's when they're most active. But they're also more dangerous at night. On one trip to Venezuela, my guide and I found a baby black caiman on the bank of a pond. It was a very exciting find as the species is nearly extinct. The caiman started making a shrill rasping sound while I took pictures, but we didn't realize it was a distress call to the mother. All of a sudden an adult came crashing out of the darkness towards us. I've never run so quickly in my life. 🙶

◁ Caiman eyes produce ghostly double reflections in the beam of a torch at Los Llanos, Venezuela.

△ Smothered in floating vegetation, a white caiman (*Caiman crocodilus*) keeps a lookout for prey at Los Llanos, Venezuela. By keeping most of their bodies hidden underwater, caimans can drift slowly into striking range without being seen by their prey.

Sit-and-wait predators must be good at hiding. Caiman can submerge all but their eyes in water, but the Surinam horned frog has to conceal itself on the forest floor. If mud and leaves are plentiful, it borrows the caiman's strategy, burying its body to leave only the eyes exposed. Failing that, it hunkers down and relies on its camouflage. Then it waits. When something wriggles within reach, it lurches from its hiding place and swallows the victim whole. Insects, frogs, reptiles, mice, and even small rats all disappear into its cavernous mouth.

◁ An enormous mouth allows the Surinam horned frog (*Ceratophrys cornuta*) to swallow prey up to half its size. Tambopata Reserve, Peru.

"I'd heard that Gorgona Island off Colombia was inhabited by the world's only pure blue lizard – the blue anolis – so I went in search of it. I couldn't believe my luck when, after only four days hunting, I spotted this rare gem, it's sapphire coat unlike anything I'd seen before. But I wasn't the only one watching it. I'd taken only two photographs when a basilisk shot out of the undergrowth, seized the anolis by the head and broke its neck. Basilisks are not native to Gorgona, they were brought there by people. Sadly, the blue anolis will probably be extinct soon because of them."

▽ ▷ A blue anolis lizard (*Anolis gorgonae*) falls victim to a basilisk (*Basiliscus galeritus*) on Gorgona Island off the coast of Colombia.

◁ An adept climber, the green vine snake (*Oxybelis fulgidus*) can extend its pencil-thin body across empty space to sneak up on unwary lizards without touching their perch and alerting them. Tambopata Reserve, Peru.

Though all snakes have the same stripped-down, streamlined form, their hunting and killing techniques vary enormously. Some twine through the vegetation following the scent of birds' nests, frogs' eggs, or sleeping lizards. Others probe burrows on the forest floor, lurk next to flowers waiting to ambush hummingbirds, or dangle from branches pretending to be vines. Scent and vision are their most important senses, but pit vipers can also "see" the warmth of prey at night by using heat-seeking pits found on the snout. With no limbs, most snakes rely on their bite to kill. The bite of the coral snake also delivers a nerve agent that paralyses a victim's lungs and muscles. Vipers inject their prey with a potent venom that attacks the blood. Constrictors have no need for venom as they kill by asphyxiation, coiling around prey and tightening each time the victim exhales.

△ The green vine snake can separate its jaw bones so that it can swallow prey wider than its own body. Backward-pointing fangs help ratchet the meal deep into the snake's gullet. Tambopata Reserve, Peru.

△ Treesnake (*Chironius*), Manú National Park, Peru.

△ Blunt-headed treesnake (*Imantodes cenchoa*),
El Avila National Park, Venezuela.

△ Rainforest hognosed pitviper (*Porthidium nasutum*),
Corcovado National Park, Costa Rica.

△ Red-eyed treesnake (*Siphlophis compressus*),
Corcovado National Park, Costa Rica.

△ Common boa (*Boa constrictor*), French Guiana.

△ Wagler's pitviper (*Tropidolaemus wagleri*),
Bako National Park, Borneo.

△ Common boa (*Boa constrictor*),
Gorgona Island, Colombia.

△ Wagler's pitviper (*Tropidolaemus wagleri*),
Bako National Park, Borneo.

“ I photographed the yellow eyelash pitviper with the greatest possible care, working silently and slowly. It's a defensive creature and will bite if irritated. Its venom is packed with enzymes that attack blood and body tissues, causing a slow death in prey such as birds and mice. It takes a very large dose to kill a person, but a moderate amount can leave you collapsed in fits of vomiting and diarrhoea. The snake lives in trees, so bites to people are often on the hands or face. The wounds swell into horrible sores that frequently become gangrenous, making amputation necessary. ”

◁ Eyelash pitvipers (*Bothriechis schlegelii*) are usually mottled green or brown, but some are a vivid golden-yellow. Tortuguero National Park, Costa Rica.

boggy cloud forests, plants have difficulty getting nutrients from the stagnant soil. Some plants have solved this problem by becoming carnivorous. Pitcher plants drown prey in fluid-filled jugs – pitchers – that develop on the tips of leaf tendrils. A fragrant nectar entices insects to the rim of the plant, where they lose their footing, and tumble in. The inner walls of the pitcher are covered with downward pointing hairs, which prevent the insects from climbing out. The water inside the pitcher plant contains a chemical that destroys its surface tension, allowing the fluid to penetrate the insect's breathing tubes and drown it.

◁▽ Pitcher plants, such as *Nepenthes villosa,* have a ridged outer surface that guides insects up to the slippery rim. Kinabalu National Park, Borneo.

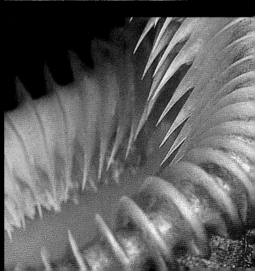

Many pitchers, including those of *Nepenthes singalana*, are equipped with lids to stop rain from diluting the digestive fluids within. Kerinci Seblat National Park, Sumatra.

△▷ The sundew plant (*Drosera binata)*, from eastern Australia, traps insects in a honey-like compound of acids and enzymes. The captive's writhing causes the plant to make more of the adhesive substance, sealing its victim's fate. Digestive enzymes break down the insect's flesh, releasing nutrients that the plant can absorb.

The strangler fig may not be a predator, but it is certainly a killer. It starts life in the canopy, its sticky seed dropped on a branch in an animal's faeces. On sprouting, it puts out an aerial root that heads straight for the ground and then digs in. Drawing on this new source of nutrients, the fig grows with increased vigour, producing ever more roots that wind around the tree and graft together, enveloping the trunk in a lattice. The fig's foliage smothers the crown and starves the tree of light, eventually killing it. Over time, the tree rots away entirely, leaving the fig's wickerwork trunk standing alone.

▷ Strangler figs (*Ficus*) grow in rainforests throughout the world, including northeast Australia (left) and Indonesia (right).

arms & armour

Many rainforest species are equipped with physical or chemical defences – the products of an arms race that has lasted millions of years.

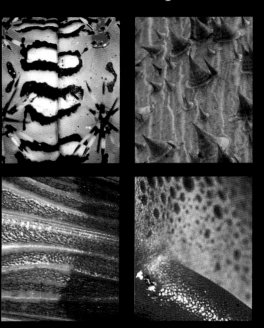

In an environment as rich in life as a rainforest, defence against predators, parasites, and other biological hazards is paramount. Plants and animals alike must protect themselves with physical or chemical weapons if they are to repel their enemies and survive. Leaf-eaters are active all year round in evergreen forests, which means plants must defend themselves continuously. Many do so by synthesizing natural pesticides: noxious, or indigestible compounds that render their tissues inedible. Evidence of this defensive strategy is always close at hand; scratched bark may ooze a toxic, milky latex, crushed leaves exude the almond-like odour of cyanide. But over time animals may evolve a resistance to specific compounds and sequester them for their own protection, driving an evolutionary arms race between plant and plant-eater. The logic of chemical deterrence also applies to the animal world, but here natural selection favours

△ Male rhinoceros beetles (Dynastinae) use their horns to battle with rivals. Manú National Park, Peru. ▷ A harlequin frog (*Atelopus flavescens*) displays its bright warning colours in the rainforests of French Guiana.

vibrant colours as a warning sign. While most rainforest animals are elusive, those with chemical defences can seem remarkably bold and self-assured – their bodies hold some of the most potent poisons found in the natural world.

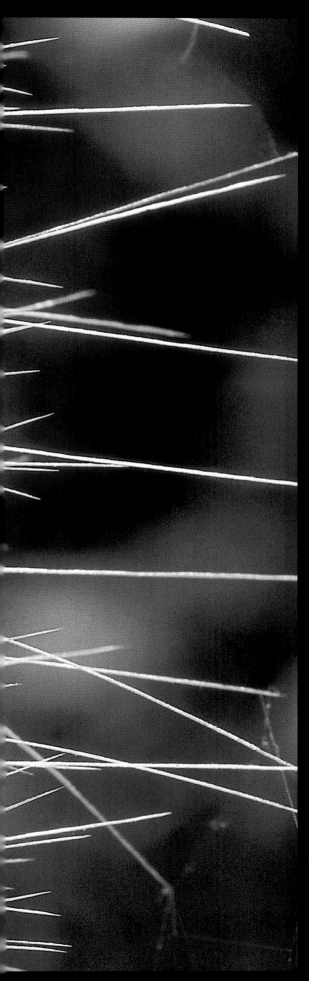

> Rattans are the cause of many an injury. They are members of the palm family but grow as vines rather than trees and tend to scramble over other plants or snake along the ground, which makes them easy to bump into. Many have razor-sharp spines that tear through clothes and flesh if you brush against them and can pierce the sole of a shoe like a knife through butter if you're unlucky enough to tread on them. Vicious though they are, the spines are not primarily defensive weapons – they serve mainly as grappling hooks that support the plant as it climbs. "

◁ The stem of a hairy Mary (*Calamus australis*) bristles with sharp spines. Daintree National Park, Queensland, Australia.

△ Rattan palm (*Plectocomia*), Daintree National Park, Queensland, Australia.

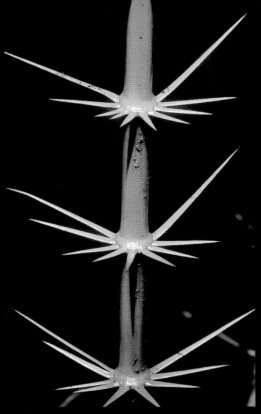

△ Rattan palm (*Plectocomia*), Kubah National Park, Borneo.

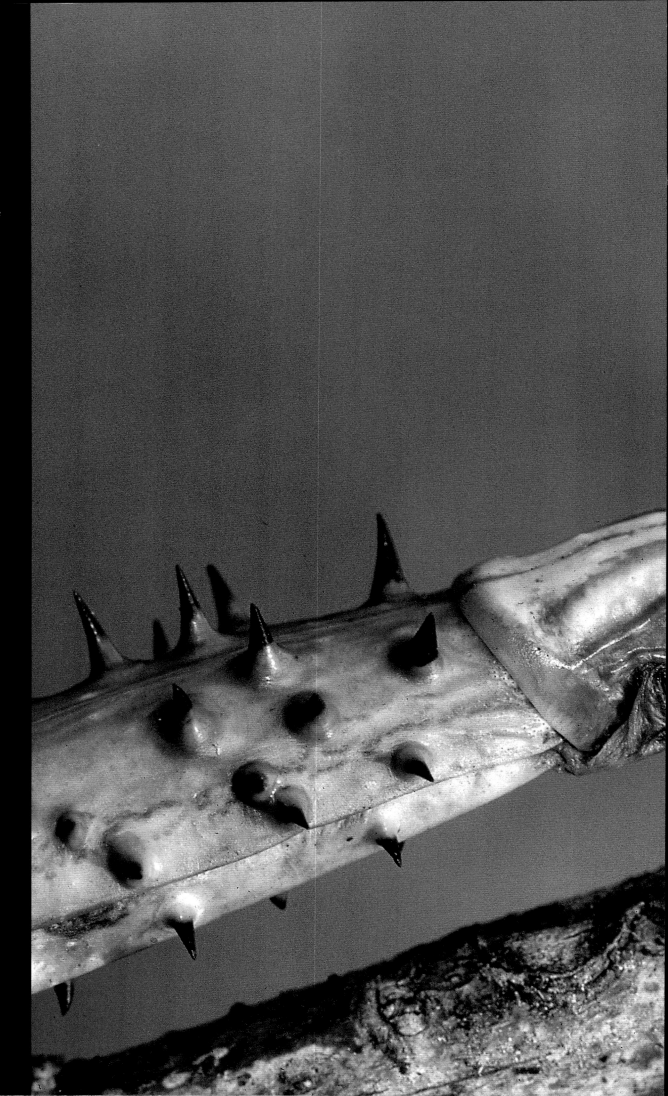

The first line of defence for many animals is body armour. Insects have skeletons on the outside of the body, forming a tough barrier to both predators and parasites. In some stick insects and many grasshoppers, defensive spines grow out of the external skeleton. Animals that try to chew on them are liable to get a nasty surprise and spit them out. Beetles (overleaf) not only have a tough external skeleton but cover themselves with a shield formed from their wing cases.

▷ Spines not only deter predators but help camouflage this stick insect (Phasmatidae) among plants. Andasibe, Madagascar.

△ Fungus beetle (Erotylidae),
Saül, French Guiana.

△ Beetle (Coleoptera),
Santa Rosa National Park, Costa Rica.

△ Fungus beetle (Erotylidae), Tambopata Reserve, Peru.

△ Fungus beetle (Erotylidae),
Manú National Park, Peru.

△ Beetle (Coleoptera),
Tambopata Reserve, Peru.

◁ The horned tortoise beetle (*Omocerus*) shields itself with
camouflaged wing cases. Many tortoise beetles can change
colour at will by squeezing a film of water under their shells.
Bico Bonita National Park, Honduras.

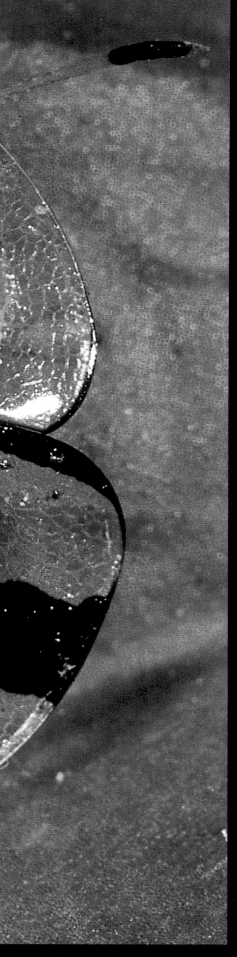

◁ △ Tortoise beetles
Aspidomorpha miliaris, Harau
Canyon Reserve, Sumatra and
Cassidinae, Tijuca National Park,
Brazil. Tortoise beetles respond to
danger by withdrawing the head
and feet like a tortoise and sealing
their flat-edged shield to the leaf.

Bright colours warn animals not to touch slug caterpillars (Limacodidae), which bristle with spines that sting like nettles. Crater Mountain, Papua New Guinea.

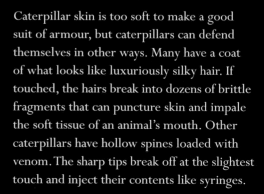

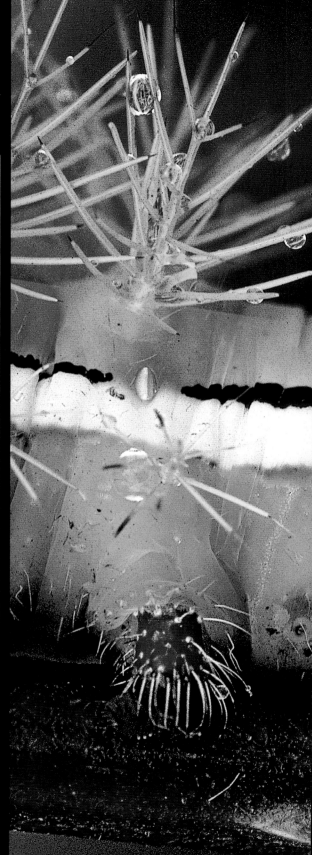

Caterpillar skin is too soft to make a good suit of armour, but caterpillars can defend themselves in other ways. Many have a coat of what looks like luxuriously silky hair. If touched, the hairs break into dozens of brittle fragments that can puncture skin and impale the soft tissue of an animal's mouth. Other caterpillars have hollow spines loaded with venom. The sharp tips break off at the slightest touch and inject their contents like syringes.

△▷ The spines of *Automeris* caterpillars inject a potent venom, producing instant, excruciating pain. Manú National Park, Peru.

△ Lymantriid caterpillar (Lymantriidae), Manú National Park, Peru.

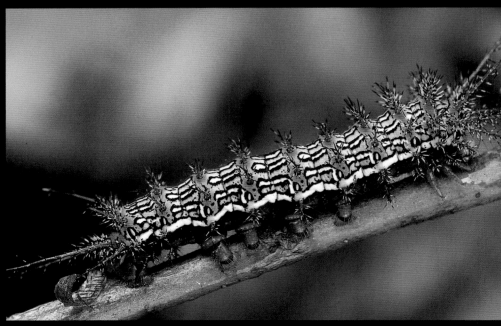

◁△ Saturniid moth caterpillar (Saturniidae), Manú National Park, Peru.

◁△ Saturniid moth caterpillar (Saturniidae), Manú National Park, Peru.

△ Caterpillar (Lepidoptera), Manú National Park, Peru.

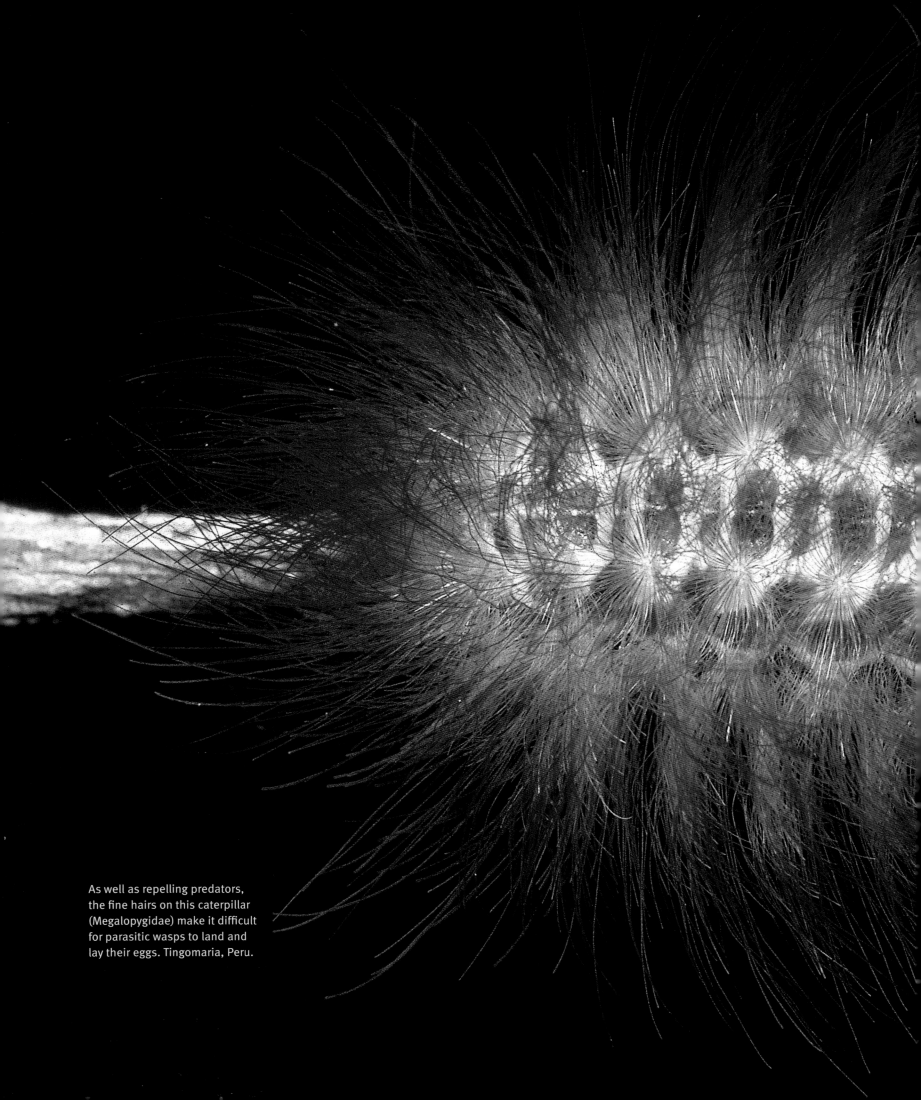

As well as repelling predators, the fine hairs on this caterpillar (Megalopygidae) make it difficult for parasitic wasps to land and lay their eggs. Tingomaria, Peru.

Another way that caterpillars can defend themselves is to steal chemical weapons. Many caterpillars have an evolved resistance to the chemical defences of their food plants. Such caterpillars not only feed with impunity but can turn the weapons to their own advantage by storing the poisons in their body. When caterpillar becomes butterfly, the chemicals may continue to defend it or the adult may start manufacturing the poisons itself. Heliconid and Actinote butterflies use both these strategies to fend off birds with cyanide and other poisons. Potent though these compounds are, they only work as a deterrent if predators are warned before they strike. Consequently, these butterflies have colours that stand out brightly to birds, such as vibrant red or yellow against black. Not all such butterflies and moths are poisonous, though. Some are harmless mimics that evolved the same pattern because of the protection it brings.

◁ When touched, this Actinote butterfly (*Actinote momina*) exudes an acrid froth that contains cyanide. Manú National Park, Peru.

△ Heliconid butterfly (*Heliconius charitonia*), Alluriquin, Ecuador.

△ Heliconid butterfly (*Heliconius melpomene*), Tambopata Reserve, Peru.

△ Actinote-mimicking moth (Hesperiidae, left) with Actinote butterfly. Manú National Park, Peru.

△ Actinote butterfly (*Actinote demonica*), Misahualli, Ecuador.

△ Heliconius-mimicking moth (Pericopidae), Manú National Park, Peru.

△ Heliconid butterfly (Heliconiidae), French Guiana.

The caterpillars of most glasswing butterflies feed on plants of the deadly nightshade family. Such plants ward off herbivores with nerve poisons like nicotine and atropine, but glasswing caterpillars are immune and store the chemicals for their own protection. In some species, however, glasswings collect their toxins as adults by visiting flowers with poisonous nectar. The males of these species use the chemicals not just for defence but as a scent to attract females.

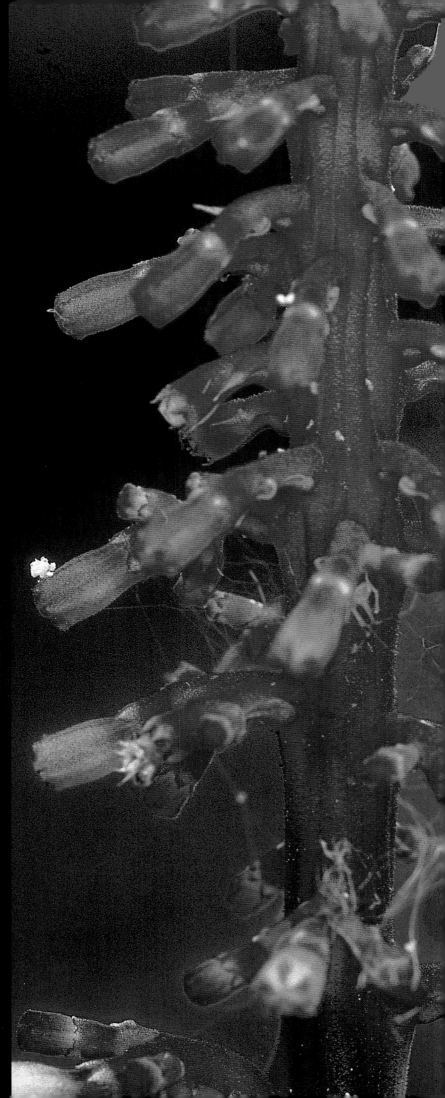

▷ Glasswing butterflies such as *Ithomia* are named for their delicate, transparent wings. Some species have become inedible by drinking poisonous nectar. Tingomaria, Peru.

△ Glasswing butterfly (Ithomiinae), Tingomaria, Peru.

△ Glasswing butterfly (Ithomiinae), Tingomaria, Peru.

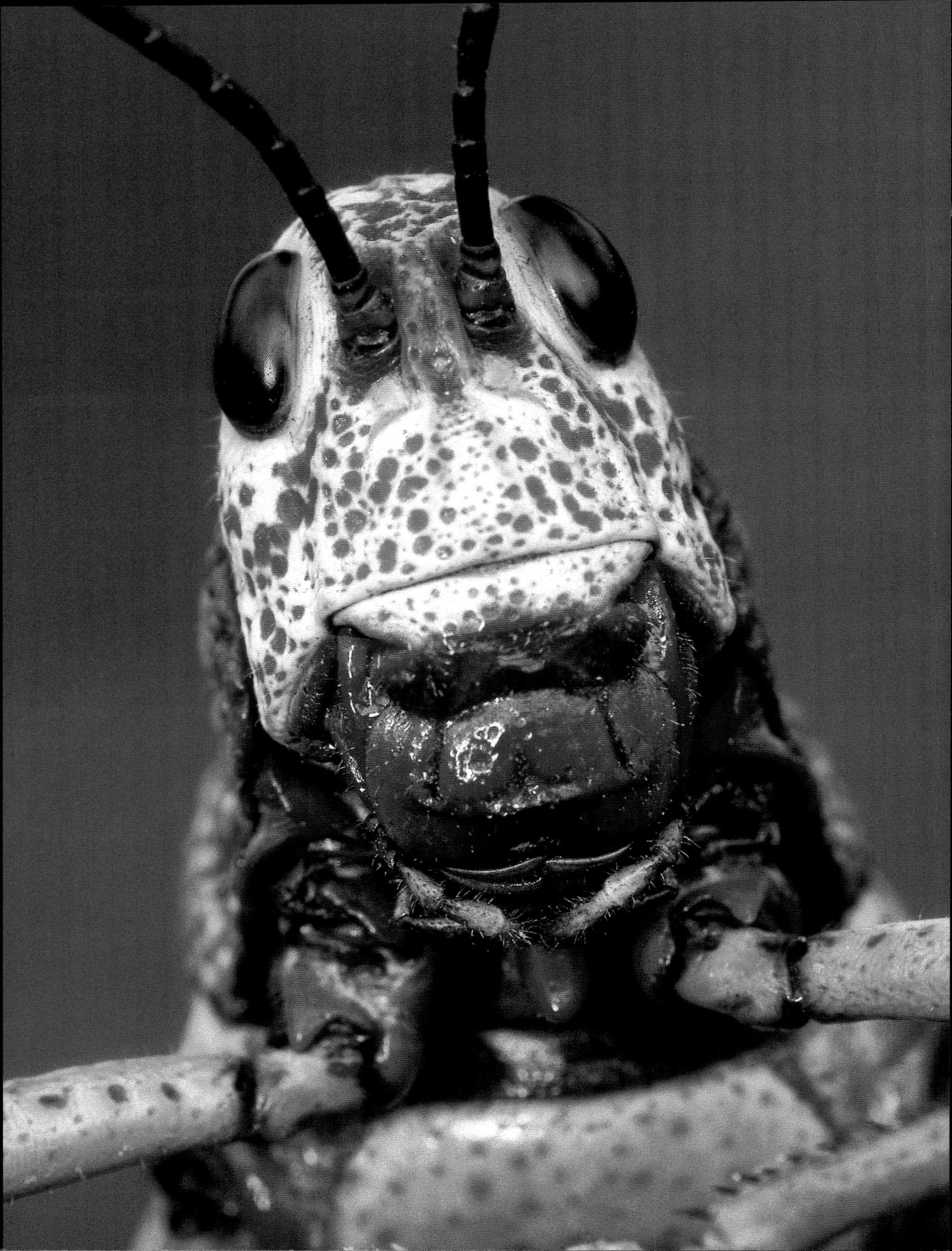

The better an animal's defences, the more nonchalant it is likely to appear. Poisonous butterflies such as heliconids and glasswings have a languid, floating style of flight that shows off their sparkling colours and makes them seem indifferent to danger. Likewise, many of the brightly coloured grasshoppers that live in rainforests seem lethargic and tame compared to their jumpy and elusive green relatives. And for good reason: their conspicuous colours warn of foul-tasting chemical defences. Animals that try to eat them have been seen to vomit afterwards, and presumably learn not to touch them again.

◁▽ Few predators can stomach grasshoppers such as *Aplatacris colorata*, which defends itself with bitter chemicals. Piura, Peru.

Dazzlingly bright warning colours help these monkey grasshoppers (Eumastacidae) to protect themselves from attack. Should the warning fail, powerful hind legs provide a means of escape. Virolin National Park, Colombia.

△ Grasshopper (*Coscineuta coxalis*),
Chocó, Colombia.

△ Grasshopper (*Syntomacris*),
Manú National Park, Peru.

△ Grasshopper (Orthoptera),
Leticia, Colombia.

△ Grasshopper (Orthoptera),
Tambopata Reserve, Peru.

△ Grasshopper (*Ommatolampis*),
Tingomaria, Peru.

△ Grasshopper (*Tropidacris cristata*),
Corcovado National Park, Costa Rica.

△ Monkey grasshopper (Eumastacidae),
Virolin National Park, Colombia.

△ Locust (*Erucius*),
Gunung Mulu National Park, Borneo.

△ Grasshopper (*Poecilocleus*),
Manú National Park, Peru.

△ Grasshopper (Eumastacinae),
Manú National Park, Peru.

destroying proteins like those in cobra venom. The venom is normally used to paralyze prey but can also be turned against predators.

◁ Plant bugs (Miridae) emit the rancid, almond-like odour of cyanide when handled. Amacayacu National Park, Colombia.

△ Stink bug (*Edessa rufomarginata*), Braulio Carillo National Park, Costa Rica.

△ Assassin bug (*Eulyes*), Gunung Gading National Park, Borneo.

△ Stink bug (Heteroptera), Tambopata Reserve, Peru.

△ Stink bug (Heteroptera), Tambopata Reserve, Peru.

frogs, which secrete paralyzing nerve agents into their damp skin. More than 100 different toxins are found in these frogs, the most deadly of which is an alkaloid called batrachotoxin, found in the poison dart frog *Phyllobates terribilis* of Colombia's Pacific rainforest. Reputed to be lethal to the touch, this frog packs enough punch to kill 50 people and is used by Native Americans to tip blowpipe darts. Poison dart frogs do not manufacture the toxins from scratch but seem to depend on a diet of ants that feed on poisonous plants.

▷ With heart-stopping colours to advertise its deadly defences, the strawberry poison frog (*Dendrobates pumilio*) can walk boldly about the forest floor during the day, when other frogs stay hidden. Braulio Carillo, Costa Rica.

△ Golden mantella (*Mantella aurantiaca*), Andasibe, Madagascar.

△ Harlequin poison frog (*Dendrobates histrionicus*), Farallones de Cali, Colombia.

△ Harlequin frog (*Atelopus spurrelli*), Chocó, Colombia.

△ Harlequin frog (*Atelopus zeteki*), El Valle de Anton, Panama.

△ Harlequin poison frog (*Dendrobates histrionicus*), Risaralda, Colombia.

△ Green and black poison frog (*Dendrobates auratus*), Cahuita National Park, Costa Rica.

△ Yellow-banded poison frog (*Dendrobates leucomelas*), Los Llanos, Venezuela.

△ Poison frog (*Allobates femoralis*),

△ Poison frog (*Dendrobates biolat*),

194

△ Strawberry poison frog (*Dendrobates pumilio*), Bocas del Toro, Panama.

△ Strawberry poison frog (*Dendrobates pumilio*), Bocas del Toro, Panama.

△ Strawberry poison frog (*Dendrobates pumilio*), Bocas del Toro, Panama.

△ Strawberry poison frog (*Dendrobates pumilio*), Bocas del Toro, Panama.

△ Strawberry poison frog (*Dendrobates pumilio*), Bocas del Toro, Panama.

△ Strawberry poison frog (*Dendrobates pumilio*), La Selva, Costa Rica.

△ Dyeing poison frog (*Dendrobates tinctorius*), Kaw, French Guiana.

△ Harlequin frog (*Atelopus erythropus*), Manú National Park, Peru.

The colours of poison frogs vary enormously, even within one species. Strawberry poison frogs, despite their name, can be red, blue, green, orange, yellow, red and blue, red and white, green and yellow, red with white spots, and so on. Six different colour variations are shown here.

△▷ Harlequin frogs such as
Atelopus spumarius are also
called clown frogs because of
their comical colours and fearless
antics. Saül, French Guiana.

deception

Visual tricks such as camouflage and mimicry help rainforest animals blend in with their environment and elude or confuse their enemies.

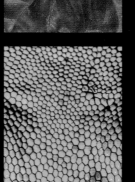

Animals without chemical defences must evade predators by other means. Many are reliant on camouflage, their bodies disguised by cryptic colours, disruptive patterns, or mimicry of inedible matter. Discovering such creatures requires sharp eyes, patient observation, and luck. A dead leaf might flutter up from the ground cover in defiance of gravity, flashing wings of fiery orange and black. A length of bark might scuttle down a tree before freezing and dissolving again.

Or a stick might suddenly come to life, rocking its matchstick body in rhythmic imitation of a twig caught in the breeze. Leaves, bark, excrement, moss, rock, lichen, water, light, and shade are all used as templates for the camouflage of rainforest animals. The illusion requires immobility, so disguised animals must resist the desire to flee until danger is close. Even then they may persevere in their act, tumbling to the forest floor like detritus and resting motionless

△ A Malaysian orchid mantis (*Hymenopus coronatus*) is disguised as a pink flower.
▷ In Borneo's forests *Phenacephorus* stick insects assume the colour and texture of moss.

where they land. Camouflage is not the only form of optical trickery used to confound an assailant. Predators often attack the head of an animal first to ensure a swift death, so fake heads and false eyes, often located far from vital organs, can provide life-saving decoys.

trunk in broad daylight requires exceptionally good camouflage. The animal must not only match the texture and colour of bark perfectly but must somehow conceal the shadow around its body, otherwise its outline will be obvious. Certain species of leaf-tailed gecko have a frill of scaly skin around the chin, legs, and abdomen that lies flat on the bark, concealing the body outline so effectively that the gecko leaf-shaped tails also help, and to complete the illusion the eyes are camouflaged too. Like many camouflaged animals, leaf-tailed geckos are active only at night and rest motionless during the day. They choose their hiding places with care, selecting a tree that best suits the gecko's individual patterning, and aligning any dark or pale patches on the body with corresponding patches of bark, lichen, or moss.

◁ A camouflaged leaf-tailed gecko (*Uroplatus*) rests upside down on a tree at Ankarafantsika National Park, Madagascar.

△ Disturbed from hiding, a leaf-tailed gecko (*Uroplatus fimbriatus*) tries to ward off danger with a wide-mouthed hiss.

△ The leaf-tailed gecko's
(*Uroplatus sikorae*) eerie
camouflage is so effective
that even when it rears up it
is easily mistaken for a branch.

▷ A transparent scale protects
the leaf-tailed gecko's eyes. It has
no eyelids, and must clean its eyes
with a flick of the tongue. Mantadia
National Park, Madagascar.

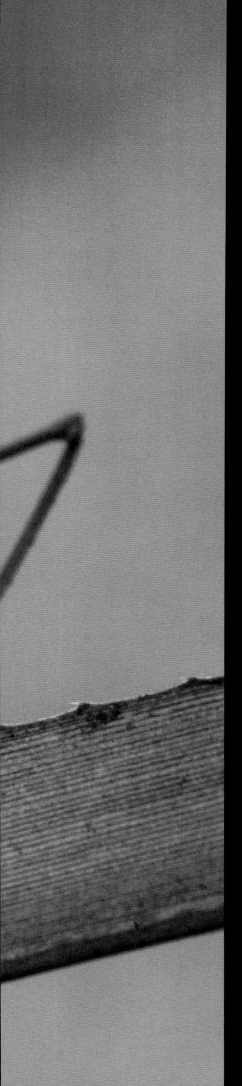

" With his cheery smile and pop-out eyes, this jumping stick looked like a character from a Disney cartoon. I almost expected him to start talking. To get a really good shot I had to stand on a nest of fire ants, though I didn't realize it at the time. Trousers are no protection against these nasty little insects and hordes of them rushed up my legs before I knew what was happening. The sting is a double-whammy. First they bite your skin with their jaws to anchor themselves, then they drive in the sting. My skin was burning all day long. A day later my legs were pink and covered with puss-filled spots. It took a fortnight to recover. "

◁ The jumping stick (*Apioscelis*) looks like a stick insect but is actually a kind of grasshopper that has evolved the same form of camouflage independently. Tambopata Reserve, Peru.

△ With its forelegs and antennae (upper left) held together and its back end raised, a stick insect (Phasmatidae) becomes a replica of a broken twig. Wooroonooran National Park, Australia.

Context is everything for the camouflaged. While tree dwellers sport the rough, knotty textures of bark or the glossy greens of foliage, inhabitants of the forest floor borrow the dark, earthy tones of compost and rotting leaves. Flat colours and rounded bodies would stand out against the jumbled litter, so these animals disguise their outlines with disruptive, angular shapes and mottled colours that mimic the pattern of light and shade.

△ Rough texture and irregular shape help disguise this grasshopper on the forest floor. Tijuca National Park, Brazil.

▷ Black spots on a bat-faced toad (*Bufo typhonius*) mimic holes in dead leaves. Amacayacu National Park, Colombia.

◁ This Malayan horned frog (*Megophrys nasuta*) is disguised as leaf litter. Its "horns" mimic leaf tips and help conceal the large eyes.

△ A mossy rock provides an ideal lookout at night, when camouflage is less important. By day the horned frog hides

Well-camouflaged animals face a dilemma: they must be inconspicuous to predators but conspicuous to potential mates. Frogs and katydids solve this problem by using sound rather than vision to advertise their presence to mates. Butterflies, however, use visual signals in courtship and so must walk a tightrope between hiding and being seen. Many species have cryptic colours on the undersides of the wings – by landing and folding their wings, they disappear. Often the shimmering colours of the upper wing-surface are caused by iridescence, an optical trick that works best in direct sunlight. Simply by flying into the shade, these butterflies lose their eye-catching sparkle, and vanish in the gloom.

△ With its wings closed, an obrina olivewing (*Nessaea*) hides its brash colours and becomes a leaf. Tambopata Reserve, Peru.

◁△ Iole's daggerwing (*Marpesia iole*) imitates a dead leaf when it closes its wings, concealing its vibrant colours. Risaralda, Colombia.

△ Stripes of magenta and blue are replaced by cocoa brown when a leafwing butterfly (*Anaea nessus*) is resting. Manú National Park, Peru.

The net-veined wings and bristly legs of this katydid duplicate the elaborate shapes and hues of the lichen on which it feeds. Chiripo National Park, Costa Rica.

Every stage in the life of a leaf is depicted by rainforest animals, from tender new leaves erupting from a bud to the mouldy remains scattered on the ground. Among the best leaf mimics are the katydids and leaf bugs. Katydids incorporate exquisite details into their disguises, such as branching patterns of leaf veins, blemishes that simulate spots of mould or insect damage, and the pointed "drip tips" that channel raindrops off the leaves. No two katydids are alike, and even members of the same species may range in appearance from the vibrant green of fresh growth to the withered brown of a dying leaf.

△ A predator could mistake this immature katydid for a scarred bud with new leaves emerging. Amacayacu National Park, Colombia.

△ Fake blemishes and a chewed corner add realism to this katydid's camouflage. Crater Mountain, Papua New Guinea.

△ The tapering, oval shape of this leaf katydid is typical of many rainforest leaves. Saül, French Guiana.

△ Only the inappropriate perch gives away these leaf bugs (*Phromnia*) in Ankarafantsika National Park, Madagascar.

Complete with leaf veins, drip tip, specks of mould, and legs like sappy stalks, a leaf katydid (*Roxelana*) is almost indistinguishable from the real thing. Manú National Park, Peru.

ecstatic and couldn't stop myself from taking pictures. Then something amazing happened. The insect raised its abdomen and displayed not just a pair of eyespots but what looked like a mouth and nose as well – a caricature of a human face. **"**

◁△ Walking leaves (Phyllidae) are closely related to stick insects and are found in the forests of Southeast Asia. Crater Mountain, Papua New Guinea.

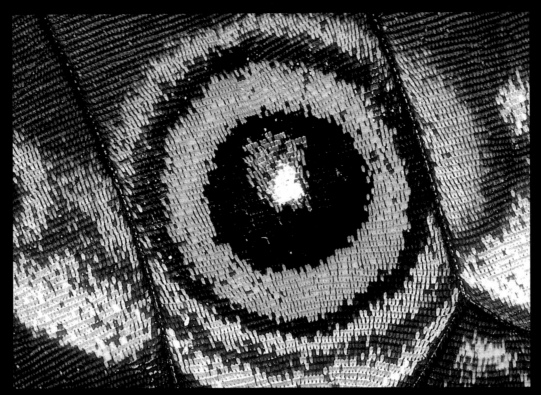

△ Morpho butterfly (*Morpho*),
Manú National Park, Peru.

Camouflage is not the only way to fool a predator. Even as an attacker strikes, an animal can bluff its way to freedom. Frogs and chameleons sometimes swell up like balloons, cheating death by appearing too big to swallow. Many moths and butterflies confuse their assailants with attention-grabbing fake eyes. Their main predators are birds, which hunt by vision and aim pecks towards the eyes as they try to snatch the head. Eyespots divert pecks away from vital organs, giving prey a second chance.

▷ The concentric circles on the hind wings of the silky owl (*Taenaris catops*) bear a striking resemblance to eyes. Crater Mountain, Papua New Guinea.

220

△ Metalmark butterfly (*Semomesia*),
Manú National Park, Peru.

△ *Mesosemia capanaea*,
Relais de Patawa, French Guiana.

△ Blue satyr (*Chloreuptychia arnaea*),
Corcovado National Park, Costa Rica.

△ Saturniid moth (*Automeris*),
Tambopata Reserve, Peru.

△ Saturniid moth (*Automeris*),
Carara Reserve, Costa Rica.

△ *Mesosemia telegone*,
Risaralda, Colombia.

◁△ Owl butterflies such as
Caligo illioneus are so-named
because their huge eyespots
look like owls' eyes. Despite the
resemblance, predators are not
deterred as these butterflies are
often found with holes in the wings
where birds have pecked at the
eyes. Tambopata Reserve, Peru.

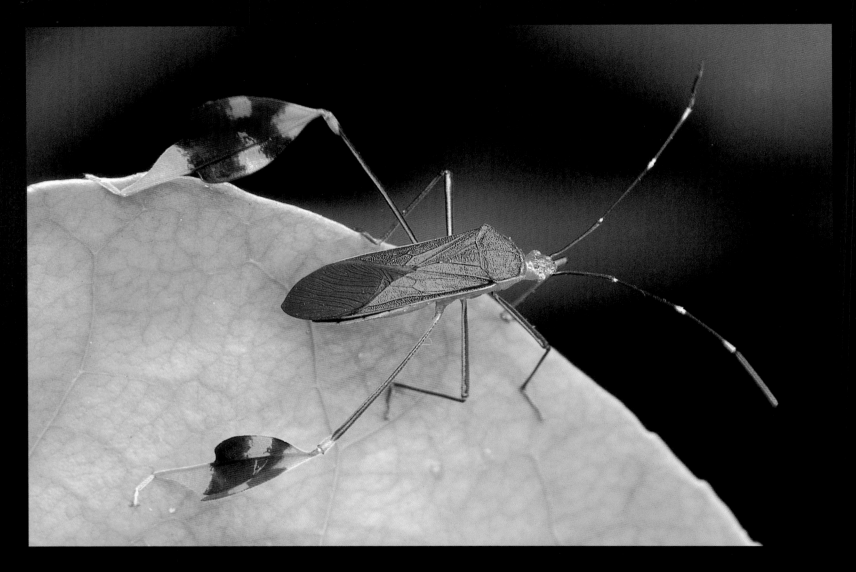

△▷ If losing a wing is preferable to losing a head, then so is losing a leg. This is probably why leaf-footed bugs such as *Anisoscelis foliacea* and *Diactor bilineata* have eye-catching flaps on their hind legs, far from the head. A hungry bird would as likely peck at the gaudy legs as at the abdomen, giving the bug a chance to escape. Tambopata Reserve, Peru.

Another way to foil an attack is to distract a predator with a colourful or fluttery tail. Many tropical lizards have brightly coloured tails that drop off when snatched and re-grow later. The elegant tails of swallowtails and many other butterflies also work as decoys. Birds mistake them for antennae and lunge for a black patch that often lies at the base of the tail, aiming for what they think is the head. The butterfly escapes with only a part of a wing missing.

◁ The flimsy tails of fluffy tits (*Zeltus amasa*) flutter in the slightest breeze, drawing a predator's attention away from the region of the head. Taman Negara National Park, Malaysia.

△ Common Posy (*Drupadia ravindra*), Taman Negara National Park, Malaysia.

△ Jewelmark (*Helicopis cupido*), Amacayacu National Park, Colombia.

△ Fluffy tit (*Zeltus amasa*), Harau Canyon Reserve, Sumatra, Indonesia.

△ Chain swordtail (*Graphium aristeus*), Kaeng Krachan National Park, Thailand.

A green dragontail butterfly (*Lamproptera meges*) sips water rich in minerals from a sandy river bank. Cameron Highlands, Malaysia.

▷ Lantern bugs (*Fulgora*) are so named because their idiosyncratic snouts were once thought to glow in the dark. Kinabatangan River, Borneo.

△ Lantern bug (*Fulgora*), Khao Yai National Park, Thailand.

△ Lantern Bug (*Fulgora*), Harau Canyon Reserve, Sumatra, Indonesia.

△ Lantern Bug (*Fulgora*), Poring Hot Spring, Borneo.

If camouflage and decoys fail to thwart an attack, an animal may have no option but to flee. There is, however, one more visual trick that may help it evade capture: a startling flash of colour. Some animals open their mouths to reveal the brilliant pink flesh within, often hissing at the same time. The red-eyed treefrog uses its eyes. It spends daylight hours crouched asleep in a tree, eyes closed and limbs tucked under its belly. If danger threatens, the enormous eyes are revealed, startling the intruder for a split-second and so giving the frog a chance to leap away.

◁▽ An adept climber, the red-eyed treefrog uses adhesive pads on its fingertips to clamber along leaves and branches in the rainforests of Central America. Cahuita National Park, Costa Rica.

△ Red-eyed treefrog (*Agalychnis callidryas*), Cahuita National Park, Costa Rica.

Vivid stripes of blue and yellow on the red-eyed treefrog's flanks may help to confuse or startle a predator as the frog leaps to safety.

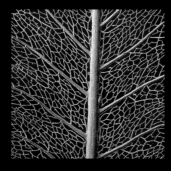

cycles

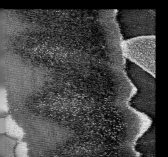    

> **" I am always amazed by the endlessly inventive ways that rainforest plants and animals find their sexual partners. "**
>
> THOMAS MARENT

The Brazil nut tree is one of the tallest and most majestic trees in the Amazon rainforest. Its straight trunk soars like a column to the top of the canopy, where it branches and spreads into a vast dome of foliage held high above the other trees. During the brief dry season, creamy yellow flowers appear among these branches and release a delicate fragrance to attract the tree's pollinators: female orchid bees. Only these jewel-like insects can pull back the tight hood covering the centre of each flower and squeeze inside to reach the nectar. As they do so, they come into contact with the flower's reproductive organs and pollinate it.

Orchid bees are indispensable in the Brazil nut's life cycle, but they are not its only partner. While the female bees are visiting the tree, the males fly to orchids to gather a special scent, without which they cannot attract the females. In doing so they pollinate the orchids. So orchids, bees, and Brazil nuts all need each other in order to reproduce.

The tangled web of relationships does not end there. Once pollinated, the tree's flowers grow into rock-hard fruits the size of coconuts. Each contains a dozen or more wedge-shaped seeds – Brazil nuts – packed like segments in an orange. The fruits drop like cannonballs to the forest floor,

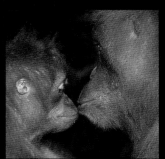

where they would sit and rot with their seeds trapped inside were it not for another helper. The agouti, a large, floor-dwelling rodent, similar in appearance to a guinea pig, is one of the only creatures that can penetrate the fruit's almost impregnable husk. It gnaws a hole to get at the nutritious nuts and eats what it can. The rest it buries, much as a squirrel conceals acorns, to see it through periods where food is in short supply. But some are forgotten, and these few, dispersed throughout the forest, become the next generation of Brazil nut trees.

The story of the brazil nut is frequently used to illustrate the fragility of the rainforest. Held together by a complex network of relationships, the ecosystem would collapse like a house of cards if any of its species were to perish. Whether or not this is actually the case, the example of the brazil nut serves to illustrate one important truth about rainforests: their inhabitants will frequently go to extraordinary lengths to reproduce.

Reproduction is the ultimate goal of every species. Mere survival is not enough. Capturing sunlight, finding food, and dodging predators are just precursors to life's most important challenge: passing on one's genes. And ways of doing so are as diverse as everything else in the rainforest. In the evolutionary hothouse, plants and animals have evolved an astonishing variety of ways to continue the cycle of life. Many, like the Brazil nut tree and its bees, have become reliant on other species to help them, their life cycles becoming intimately and inextricably entwined as they evolve together.

Death is as much a part of the cycle as sex. In the warm and humid conditions of rainforests, dead plant and animal matter is swiftly colonized by fungi, bacteria, and other agents of decay. As these organisms digest the matter, nutrients locked within it are released into the soil and recycled. Consequently, rainforests are in a perpetual state of turnover, their myriad inhabitants contributing to endless cycles of life and death.

cycles

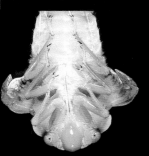

flower to fruit

Rainforest plants depend on animals as reproductive intermediaries, both to carry their pollen between flowers and to disperse seeds.

The reproductive lives of plants are governed by the seasons in most parts of the world. Spring brings a flush of new growth and flowers; summer and autumn bring fruits and seeds. In the rainforests, however, year-round warm weather enables plants to flower, fruit, and set seed when it suits them. Some species flower on an annual basis, taking their cue from the cycle of wet and dry seasons. Others do so continuously, or in response to internal stimuli which

results in cycles that last weeks, months, or years, all the members of the species synchronized so that the flowers appear together, ensuring pollination. Unlike temperate plants, many of which can self-fertilize, most rainforest plants must exchange pollen with other individuals if they are to reproduce. But finding a partner of the right species among the bewildering diversity of life is difficult, so plants recruit specialist pollinators, rewarding the animals that visit the right

△ A glasswing butterfly (Ithomiinae) drinks nectar in Manú National Park, Peru. ▷ The sex organs of the passionflower (*Passiflora*) dust hummingbirds with saffron-coloured pollen.

types of flowers and obstructing those that do not. Plants also rely on animals to disperse their seeds. Only the very tallest trees catch enough wind to risk scattering seeds in the air, so most plants instead bribe animals to transport the seeds, packaging them in tempting fruits.

△ Ground orchid (*Plocoglottis hirta*),
Niah National Park, Borneo.

△ Epiphytic orchid *(Bulbophyllum macranthum)*,
Sabah, Borneo.

△ Slipper orchid (*Paphiopedilum rothschildianum*), Sabah, Borneo.

Pollen carried to the wrong kind of flower is wasted, so it pays to employ a specialist courier. Orchids have evolved into a seemingly endless variety of forms, many of which use just a single species of insect (or one sex of one species) for pollination. Not all reward visitors with nectar. Some mimic male bees of a particular species and so elicit attacks from rivals. Others mimic sexually receptive females with much the same result. The orchid *Bulbophyllum* attract flies with the odour of rotting flesh, and lady's slipper orchids (*Paphiopedilum*) trap insects in a pouch with a single narrow exit; as they struggle out, pollen is glued to their backs.

△ Moth orchid (*Paphiopedilum lowii*),
Sabah, Borneo.

△ Epiphytic orchid (*Psychopsis papilio*),
Saül, French Guiana.

△ Epiphytic orchid (*Renanthera bella*),
Sabah, Borneo.

△ Orchid (*Liparis lacerata*),
Sabah, Borneo.

△ *Phalaenopsis amabilis* and many other orchids have a central landing platform where insects alight. Sticky packets of pollen are glued onto the visitor from above.

The colour, shape, and scent of a flower are clues to the identity of its pollinator. Vibrant colours appeal to animals with good colour vision, such as birds and butterflies. Nocturnal visitors such as bats and moths are drawn to white or creamy flowers, which are easier to see in the gloom and often produce strong scents. Dainty flowers with landing platforms are for flying insects; large flowers that dangle in open spaces are for mammals or birds. The *Heliconias* of tropical America employ hermit hummingbirds as their pollinators. With their long, curved bills, hermit hummingbirds are among the few animals that can negotiate their way into the tubular flowers hidden inside the spiky flower sheaths.

▷ The spiky red sheaths around *Heliconia* flowers serve both as a beacon to hummingbirds and a barrier to nectar-stealing bees. Manú National Park, Peru.

△ *Heliconia*, Farallones de Cali, Colombia.

△ Epiphytic orchid (*Dendrobium macrophyllum*), Crater Mountain, Papua New Guinea.

△ *Calceolaria*, Manú National Park, Peru.

△ *Eugenia*, Crater Mountain, Papua New Guinea.

△ Bromeliad (*Tillandsia ionantha*), Peninsula Paria, Venezuela.

△ Milkweed (*Asclepias curassavica*), Sabah, Borneo.

△ *Gaultheria*, Manú National Park, Peru.

△ Red mangrove (*Rhizophora mangle*), Bako National Park, Borneo.

△ Bromeliad (*Navia tentacula*), Auyan Tepui, Venezuela.

The flaming orange flowers of a monkey brush plant (*Combretum aubletii*) are a magnet to butterflies and hummingbirds. Amacayacu National Park, Colombia.

Many rainforest flowers, like this *Scadox multiflorus*, work like a brush, with pollen borne on the tips of long, flexible stamens that dust the faces of visiting animals. Kibale National Park, Uganda.

Beautiful flowers and sweet
perfumes are not the only
means of attracting pollinators.
The *Rafflesia* plant uses the
stench of death to lure carrion
flies into its amazing, flesh-
coloured blooms. As the flies
search the flower's interior for
rotting flesh in which to lay
their eggs, they blunder into its
reproductive organs and pollinate
it. *Rafflesia* is a peculiar plant.
The giant flowers are its only
visible structures, the rest of
the plant growing as a parasitic
thread inside vines. The flower
buds form where the vine runs
across the ground. Over several
days they swell to the size of
a cabbage and then unfurl their
monstrous petals, which last for
only three or four days before
collapsing into a slimy black mass

◁ *Rafflesia* flowers can reach
106 cm wide, making them the
world's largest flowers. Gunung
Gading National Park, Borneo.

△ *Xylopia* (Annonaceae), Manú National Park, Peru.

△ Fruits of flowering plant (Rubiaceae), Kerinci Seblat National Park, Sumatra.

△ *Cyrtosperma*, Gunung Mulu National Park, Borneo.

△ Fruits of flowering plant (Rubiaceae), Virolin National Park, Colombia.

△ Pico de grulla (*Gesneriasa cerulata*), Tingomaria, Peru.

△ Ripening fruits of flowering plant (Araceae), Poring Hot Spring, Borneo.

Once flowers have succeeded in obtaining pollen, the beginnings of the next generation develop inside them as seeds. Seeds must reach new locations, but there is little wind beneath the canopy to carry them. The best means of dispersal is to exploit the mobility of animals. Many rainforest plants package seeds in nutritious flesh as a bait for animal couriers, advertising the fruits with eye-catching colours and attractive scents. But animals are not always faithful dispersers — many try to consume the seeds as well. For protection, seeds may be laced with poison, encased in hard shells that only the toughest teeth can penetrate, or mixed inseparably into the fruit's flesh so that animals must swallow the lot and scatter the seeds later in droppings.

△ *Tilesia baccata*, Manú National Park, Peru.

△ Seed, Corcovado National Park, Colombia.

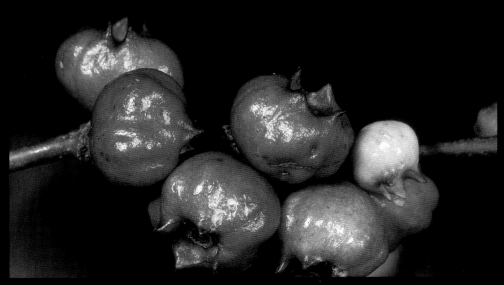

△ Fruits of flowering plant (Rubiaceae), Gunung Gading National Park, Borneo.

△ La Planada Nature Reserve, Colombia.

△ Manú National Park, Peru.

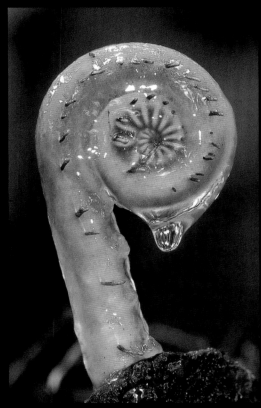

△ La Planada Nature Reserve, Colombia.

Some plants have no need for flowers, fruit, or seeds. Ferns start life as spores – microscopic particles that float on the air like dust and can ride the faint currents below the canopy. These settle everywhere and come to life wherever conditions suit them, even in the deep shade of the forest floor. In the peculiar life cycle of ferns, reproduction happens after the spores have sprouted, and the resulting embryos become a new generation of plants.

▷ Ferns (Pteridophyta) can take years to develop, coiled up inside a tight bud. When mature, they unravel and swell with moisture. Manú National Park, Peru.

lifelines

In rainforests as elsewhere, the lives of animals are governed by one force above all others: the urge to reproduce and pass on their genes.

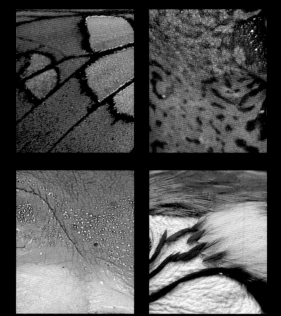

Just as the plants in a rainforest must attract pollinators, animals must locate partners of their own kind among a great diversity of species, a challenge compounded by the need to hide from predators. Communication – whether through sight, scent, or sound – is the solution, even if it entails risking exposure. The tapestry of sound that fills the rainforest at night bears witness to this overwhelming urge to find and attract a mate. While plants exchange

pollen with any compatible partner, animals must prove their suitability as mates through elaborate rituals of courtship. Usually females have the power to choose and the males must strive to impress them, flaunting the quality of their genes with extravagant ornaments, battles over territory, or acrobatic displays of strength and agility. For some animals, reproduction ends with sex. Others nurture their offspring through the perilous early

△ A chestnut-eared aracari (*Pteroglossus castanotis*), Brazil. Male and female aracaris share responsibility for raising their young.
▷ Siamang gibbons (*Hylobates syndactylus*) sing with mates to cement their bond. Singapore.

stages of life, thus increasing their chances of survival. But the logic of natural selection means that many must perish, leaving only the fortuitous and the well-adapted to mate, pass on their genes, and continue the line in turn.

Without sunlight to guide their way, nocturnal animals use scent and sound to find mates in the darkness. Each species of male frog uses a distinctive call to attract mates of the right kind. The females listen carefully as the calls also contain subtle clues about the suitors' eligibility. A deep pitch, for instance, suggests the caller is large. Some female frogs are drawn to males with the longest and most complex calls, even though such males risk being caught by frog-eating bats. Perhaps their boldness and daring are signs of good genes.

▷ Using a huge throat sac to add resonance to his calls, a male *Hyla sarayacuensis* treefrog croaks for a mate in Tambopata Reserve, Peru.

" I heard the smooth croaking of glass frogs at night and went in search, following my ears. These frogs are named for their translucent skin, which in some species you can see straight through to the bones and organs beneath. They stay near water and are often found clinging to wet rocks in waterfalls and streams or perching in the dripping vegetation nearby. Their glassy bodies are hard to see among wet leaves and it took me half an hour to spot one, but then I saw them everywhere. My guide held an umbrella while I took the pictures. "

◁▽▷ The rare glass frog (*Cochranella truebae*) lives only in the cloud forests of Manú National Park, Peru. Adults are barely 25 mm long.

For animals that are active by day, looks are hugely important. Female birds judge mates by their appearance, preferring striking looks and vibrant, healthy plumage. Over thousands of years of evolution visual signals have been exaggerated, and many tropical birds are now embellished with extravagant ornaments and dazzling colours that stand out against the backdrop of green. Aerobatic displays, and dancing, are other ways of catching the eye. Butterflies (overleaf) also inhabit a world of vision and may be able to perceive an even broader range of colours than birds. They gather in sunny clearings and flash their wings to attract mates, the bold colours and patterns allowing each species to recognize its own.

▷ In cassowaries (*Casuarius*), the females are much bigger and more brightly coloured than males. These huge, flightless birds have a protective casque on their head and neck wattles that can change colour according to the bird's mood. Lae, Papua New Guinea.

△ The resplendent quetzal (*Pharomachrus mocinno*) glows from head to foot in iridescent plumes. Only the male has long tail streamers. Cerro La Muerte, Costa Rica.

△ The Victoria crowned pigeon (*Goura victoria*) is the world's largest pigeon and as big as a turkey. Males and females both have a crown of lacy head feathers. Lae, Papua New Guinea.

△ Malay red harlequin (*Paralaxita damajanti*), Gunung Mulu National Park, Borneo.

△ Bluemark (*Lasaia meris*), Iguaçu National Park, Brazil.

△ Nymphalid butterfly (*Precis sophia*), Kibale National Park, Uganda.

△ Actinote butterfly (*Actinote momina*), Manú National Park, Peru.

△ Lampeto greenmark (*Caria lampeto*), Risaralda, Colombia.

△ Nymphalid butterfly (Nymphalidae), Virolin National Park, Colombia.

△ Mexican Fritillary (*Euptoieta hegesia*),
Camp Caiman, French Guiana.

△ Scarce bamboo page (*Philaethria dido*),
Rurrenabaque, Bolivia.

△ Eleuchia Longwing (*Heliconius eleuchia primularis*), Machalilla National Park, Ecuador.

△ Typhla Satyr (*Oressinoma typhla*),
El Avila National Park, Venezuela.

△ Painted Jezebel (*Delias hyparete*),
Chiangmai, Thailand.

△ Satyr butterfly (*Euptychia*),
Tambopata Reserve, Peru.

> Once you've seen the cock-of-the-rock's courtship dance you never forget it. It takes place at a communal dance site where up to a dozen males perform at once, fluttering their wings and bobbing their day-glo orange heads for the benefit of a watching female, who then mates with her favourite (often the same male wins every time). Photographing this spectacle was difficult. It takes place around dawn and dusk on the forest floor, where the light is poor at the best of times. I wanted to use natural light to capture the colours, so I had to use long exposures. I used up 20 rolls of film and got only a dozen sharp pictures.

◁▽▷ The male Andean cock-of-the-rock (*Rupicola peruviana*) has vivid orange or red plumage, while the females are drab and brown. Manú National Park, Peru.

Colourful plumage alone does not win a bird a mate. Males must also demonstrate their genetic superiority with song, dance, and other ritualized displays of fitness. The most colourful and elaborate courtship rituals are those of the birds of paradise and bowerbirds of New Guinea and Australia. The males of these two species contribute little but genes to the next generation and instead devote all their energies to seduction, leaving females to rear families alone. Instead of showy feathers, bowerbirds construct a stack of twigs — a bower — and decorate it with colourful ornaments, from berries and flowers to scraps of plastic. The most extravagant bower is that of the Vogelkop bowerbird. Built like a thatched hut with a conical roof, it is big enough for a person to crawl inside. The Vogelkop bowerbird dresses the area in front of the bower with neatly arranged piles of ornaments such as flowers, leaves and pebbles, each pile containing objects of exactly the same colour.

◁▽ The male satin bowerbird (*Ptilonorhynchus violaceus*) builds a thatched walkway and surrounds it with numerous trinkets that match its sapphire eyes. Females are invited into the central promenade, where the couple mate. Lamington National Park, Australia.

◁▽ In contrast to the rituals of courtship, sex for most animals is perfunctory. Elena's treefrogs (*Boophis elenae*) mate in trees, the male clasped to his partner's back. He douses her eggs with sperm as they leave her body. Ranomafana National Park, Madagascar.

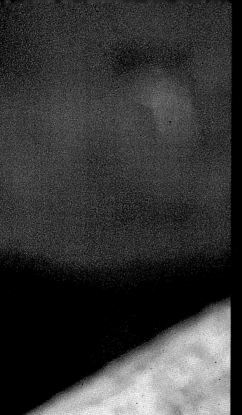

◁ Poison dart frogs such as *Epipedobates trivittatus* carry their tadpoles on their back and deposit them in temporary pools. Tambopata Reserve, Peru.

▽ Breathing through its damp skin, the tadpole of a monkey treefrog (*Phyllomedusa bicolor*) can leave its pool before it is fully developed. Tambopata Reserve, Peru.

With courtship and mating complete, the next challenge for animals is to make sure offspring survive. In temperate regions, frogs simply deposit their eggs in water and let fate do the rest. Rainforest frogs, however, are more inventive. Although their eggs must still be placed in water, as development can only occur in moist conditions, many avoid permanent pools, where eggs would probably be eaten by fish. Instead, they use temporary puddles, nests of foam, or attach their eggs to leaves which overhang water. Some frogs skip the tadpole stage altogether and the eggs turn directly into miniature froglets. Although most species abandon their eggs after laying, some are devoted parents. Poison dart frogs carry tadpoles on their back, and deposit them singly in water-filled crevices high in the trees. They go on to visit them every day, adding sterile eggs to the water for food.

To photograph the hornbill's nest in Tangkoko Nature Reserve in Sulawesi, I built a 17 m-high tower from scaffolding poles and put a camouflaged hide on top. I was in it from dawn to dusk for 10 days – more than 100 hours in total. The male hornbill visited the nest 8–10 times a day, the swoosh of his wings alerting me to his presence. But the bright sunlight was often too harsh for photographs and I kept having to wait for the next visit. Between visits there was nothing to do and I sometimes fell asleep. The first time I woke I realized with horror that there was nothing to stop me rolling off the tower, so I tied myself in. Meals were brought by my guide and hauled up by rope. Trips to the toilet involved standing precariously on the edge and listening to the inevitable croaks of frogs that mistook the sound for rain.

inside by blocking the entrance with mud. Tangkoko Nature Reserve, Sulawesi, Indonesia.

△ The female hornbill peers out of the slit in the blocked entrance hole. Hornbill mothers can spend three months imprisoned in a tree with their young.

△ Carrying a small fruit in its bill, the male hornbill prepares to deliver a meal. He must bring food to the nest several times a day or the family will starve.

Few animals make such devoted parents as orang-utan mothers (*Pongo*), who spend up to eight years looking after their young. Gunung Leuser National Park, Sumatra, Indonesia.

Hornbills, and other birds, look after their offspring for a matter of weeks, but the great apes look after theirs for years. For juvenile apes, this sheltered period of life is a time to learn vital survival skills. Infant orang-utans accompany their mothers everywhere for at least four years, watching and learning all the time. They find out how to gather up to 400 different types of food, learning which trees produce fruit and when to visit them. They learn how to make nests by folding branches, how to use their body weight to swing vines and bend trees, how to dip their fingers into tree holes to soak up water or pull out honey. They even master primitive tools, including twigs to fish for termites and wedges of wood to prise husks from fruit.

◁ △ ▷ Much like human babies, infant Sumatran orang-utans (*Pongo abelii*) cling to their mothers for the first few years of life. Gunung Leuser National Park, Sumatra, Indonesia.

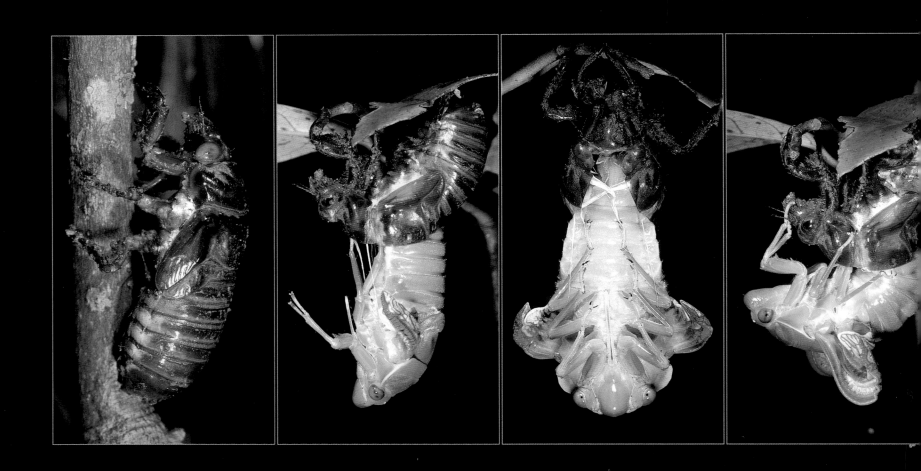

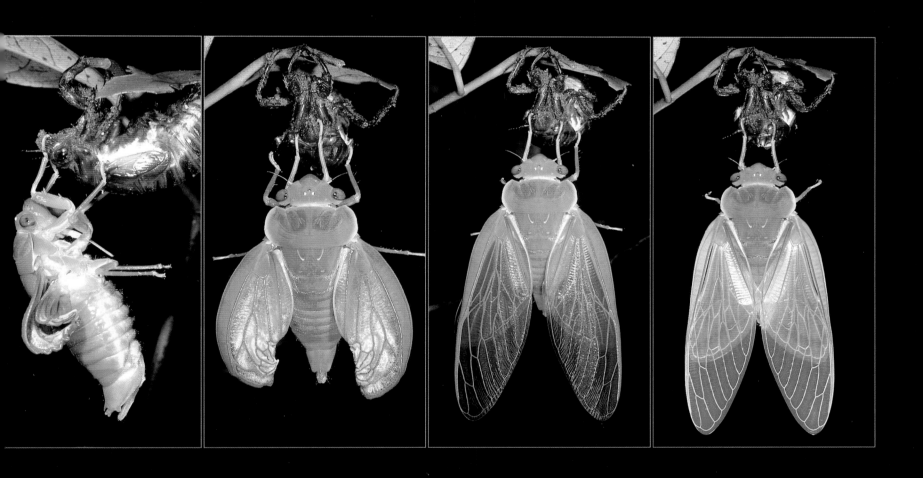

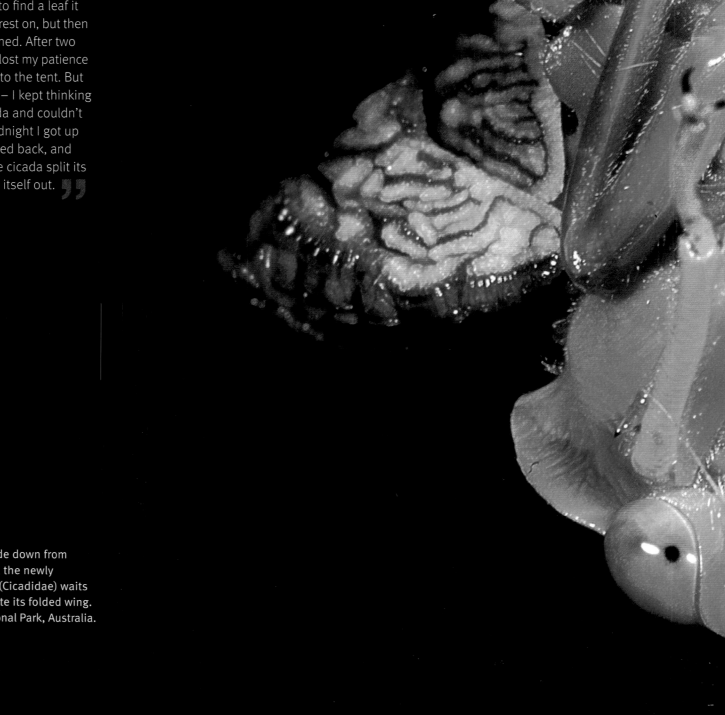

“ Cicadas spend most of their life underground as wingless nymphs, sucking juices from roots. When they're ready to become adults, they crawl out of the ground, shed their skin, and fly away transformed. I'd wanted to photograph this amazing process for years but so far had only found empty nymphal cases. My luck turned on a night walk in Australia's rainforest when I spotted a cicada nymph crawling on the ground. It took the nymph about an hour to find a leaf it was content to rest on, but then nothing happened. After two hours waiting I lost my patience and went back to the tent. But it was no good – I kept thinking about the cicada and couldn't sleep. So at midnight I got up again and walked back, and right on cue the cicada split its skin and eased itself out. ”

▷ Hanging upside down from its moulted skin, the newly emerged cicada (Cicadidae) waits for blood to inflate its folded wing. Palmerston National Park, Australia.

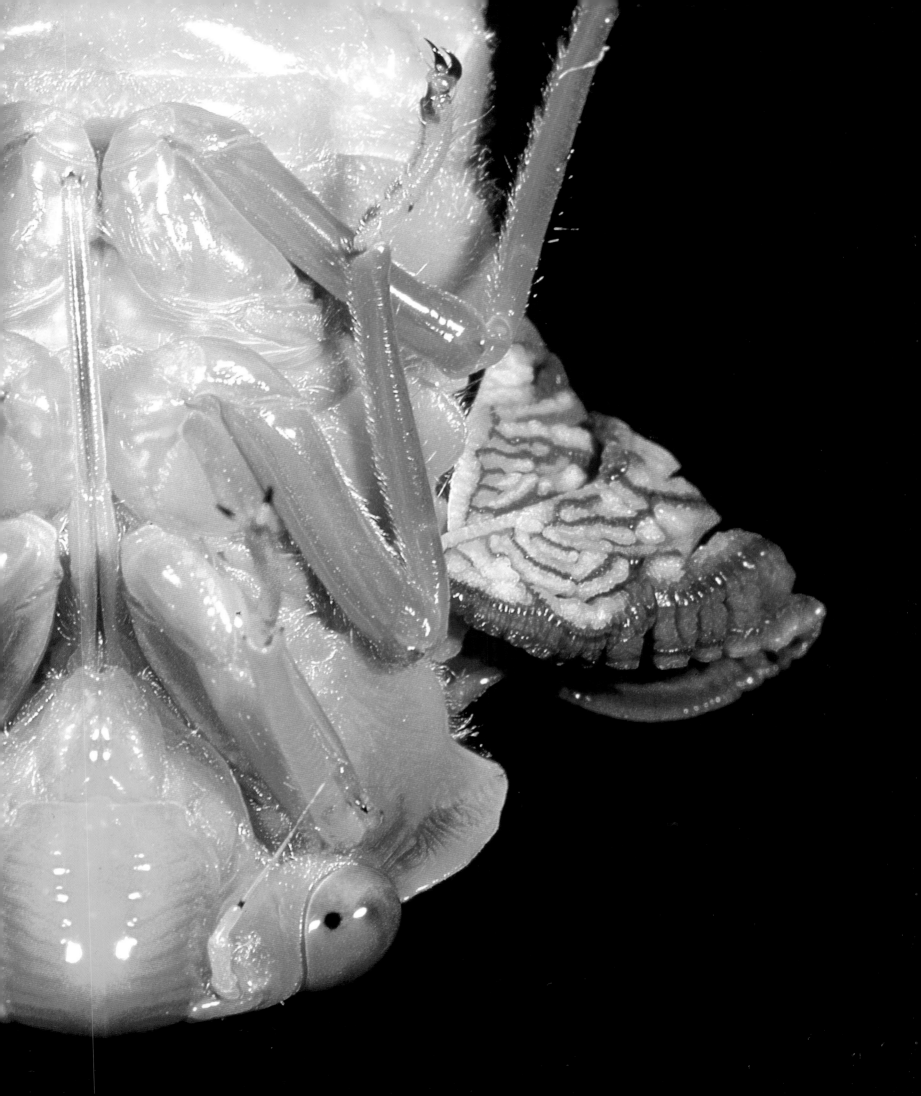

recyclers

In the rainforest the constant warmth and moisture promote the rapid decomposition of dead matter, and nutrients are soon recycled.

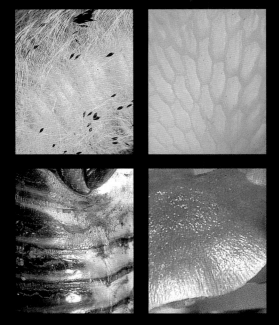

Death and decay are everywhere in a rainforest. A rain of dead organic matter – branches, leaves, seeds and fruits – falls continually to the forest floor, where the detritus becomes food for armies of scavengers. Beetles hoard excrement and termites devour wood; worms dispose of the leaves; maggots, cockroaches, and mites feast on corpses. The most important recyclers are fungi and bacteria. Working largely unseen, they infiltrate every speck of debris and digest it from within, unlocking precious nutrients by breaking chemical matter into simpler parts, and then returning them to the soil. Although none of these organisms exists to provide support for the ecosystem, their combined actions keep nutrients in cycle and the forest in balance. In the warm, wet climate of tropical rainforests, the rate at which decomposition occurs is accelerated. A leaf can break down in weeks, an entire tree within a few years. So efficient is the

△ Toadstools and seedlings emerge from leaf litter at Mission Beach, Australia.
▷ White fungus erupts from the body of a moth. Amacayacu National Park, Colombia.

process of decay that very little soil is able to accumulate on the forest floor. In places, only a thin layer of organic litter may cover the ground, with the roots of trees growing into it from below to scour the refuse for nutrients before they are washed away by the rain.

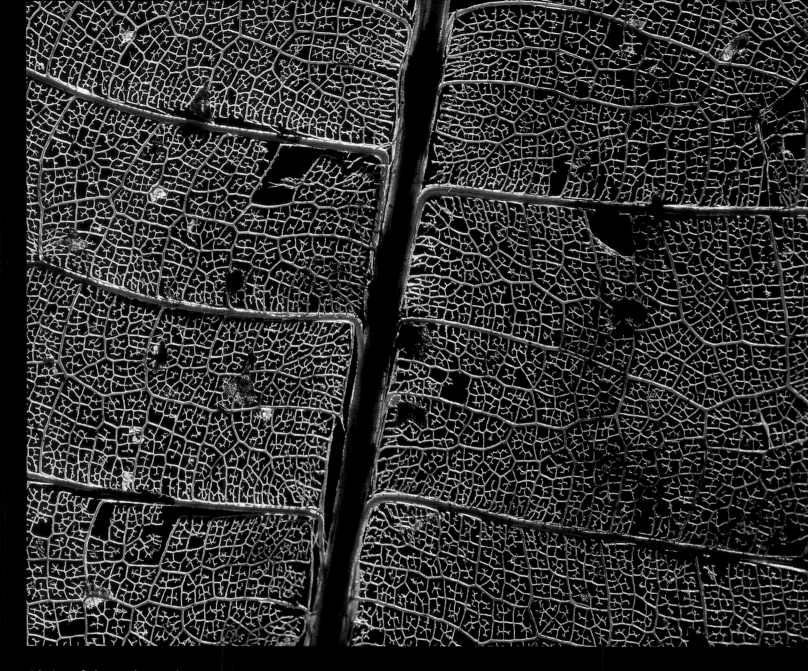

△▷ Its soft tissues devoured
by caterpillars, a leaf is reduced
to a skeleton of veins. The tough,
indigestible fibres of cellulose that
make up the skeleton will become
food for fungi on the forest floor.
Farallones de Cali, Colombia.

spores from the tips of hair-like growths. The spores drift away in the damp air to infect more victims. Other fungi help rather than hinder their hosts. The roots of most rainforest plants are surrounded and infiltrated by a fuzzy mass of fungi that help plants extract water and minerals from the impoverished soil. The symbiotic relationship that many tropical orchids have with these fungi is so important that the orchids will not even germinate unless their fungal partner is present in the soil.

▷ Killed by a parasitic fungus that spread to its antennae and along its wing veins, a moth becomes a host for the parasite's spores. Amacayacu National Park, Colombia.

Tree trunks are often riddled with fungi
at the base, even though the crown may be
lush and healthy. The fungi eat away at the
central heartwood, slowly turning the trunk
into a hollow shell. The infection can ultimately
weaken a tree to the point of collapse, but,
paradoxically, the fungi bring benefits too.
Infected trees develop inward-growing roots
that mine the rotten core for nutrients released
from the wood. The cavity also attracts ants
and termites that gather compost from the
surroundings and so fertilize the roots.

◁ Bracket fungi and mushrooms
emerge from the trunk of a rotting
tree at Tambopata Reserve, Peru.
▽ Turkey tail fungus (*Stereum ostrea*)
at Eungella National Park, Australia.

combined cells develop into "fruiting bodies"
such as mushrooms and toadstools, which
produce offspring by the million.

Orange agarics (*Mycena*),
Manú National Park, Peru.

Pink agarics (*Marasmius haematocephalus*),
Manú National Park, Peru.

Marasmius mushrooms spring to
life after heavy rain but shrivel up
and become dormant when they
dry out. Tambopata Reserve, Peru.

△ Striped agaric (*Marasmius*), Tambopata Reserve, Peru.

△ Blue agaric (*Clitocybula azurea*), Tambopata Reserve, Peru.

△ Red marasmioids, Tambopata Reserve, Peru.

△ Pink agaric (*Marasmius*), Saül, French Guiana.

△ White marasmioids, Manú National Park, Peru.

△ Bird's nest fungus (*Cyathus*), Tambopata Reserve, Peru.

△ *Polyporous tenuiculus*, Manú National Park, Peru.

△ Morel stinkhorn (*Phallus multicolor*), Mission Beach, Australia.

△ *Dacryopinax spathularia*, Mission Beach, Australia.

Unlike animals, fungi can break down the tough fibres in plants. Some rainforest insects exploit this ability by cultivating edible fungi in their nests, so turning indigestible matter into food. In Africa, termites feed wood to fungi and eat the resulting compost. In South and Central America, leafcutter ants use fragments of leaves to grow a nutritious fungus that exists nowhere else. Hidden underground, the enormous nests of leafcutters can grow larger than a house and may harbour 8 million residents.

▽▷ Leafcutter ants (*Atta*) dissect leaves and carry the fragments back to fungus gardens in their nest. Manú National Park, Peru.

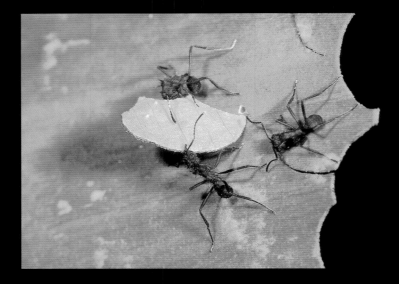

With their cargo clasped firmly in pincer-like jaws, leafcutter ants (*Atta*) make their way back to the nest in procession. Manú National Park, Peru.

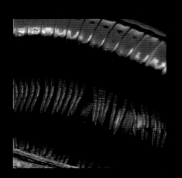

society

> # " What fascinates me most about social animals like monkeys and apes is the tension and conflict within their societies – in many ways their world is just like ours. "
>
> THOMAS MARENT

As the sun rises over the thickly forested island of Sulawesi in Indonesia the rattling chorus of nocturnal frogs and cicadas gives way to the fluid notes of birdsong. The dawn mists part abruptly and draw back like curtains, allowing hot sunlight to pour into the canopy and banish the chill of the night. A troop of black macaques stirs in its sleeping tree. Grunts, coos, and an occasional bark drift down from the branches as the monkeys begin the daily ritual of social networking. Eyes dart back and forth, exchanging nervous glances.

Teeth flash, eyebrows rise, lips smack together. Some of the females extend an affectionate hand to groom friends or relatives; other members of the troop bark tetchily at their subordinates. At last, the dominant male decides to move off into the forest. With effortless grace, he lowers his powerful frame down the tree trunk and ambles away, followed by the rest of the troop.

Living in a social group is not the norm for rainforest animals. There are no majestic herds of stampeding antelope or prides of lions.

308

In general, the animals are loners, too shy and secretive to draw attention to themselves by ganging together. Yet some not only live in conspicuous groups but have societies of great sophistication, with rules of etiquette, class systems, power struggles, and mighty leaders.

A social way of life has distinct advantages, the greatest of which is safety in numbers. Solitary animals are easy prey as they cannot watch their surroundings continuously. A group, however, has many pairs of eyes and ears and can see danger coming from all directions. When a predator is spotted, the alarm is raised and the whole group dashes for safety. Since the risk of being seen by a predator is higher in daylight, the social proclivity is pronounced in animals that are active by day. Another factor is food. Many rainforest animals subsist on a diet of fruit, which, though available all year round, tends to be patchy in distribution. Fruiting trees might be heavily laden but widely scattered, so it makes sense to forage as a group.

Some animal societies are riven with internal conflicts, inequalities, and violence. However, others are so well-organized they operate like clockwork. Social insects, such as termites and ants, live in strictly controlled societies with thousands or even millions of citizens. Most are sterile workers who share the majority of their genes with the colony's only breeding female: the queen. This close genetic relationship, and the controlling pheromones produced by the queen, foster co-operation and division of labour.

In the convoluted ecology of the rainforest, intimate relationships often develop across species divides, frequently to the mutual advantage of both sides. Plants form effective symbiotic partnerships with pollinators, seed dispersers, even with infesting armies of ants. But not all such interspecific relationships are mutually beneficial. Nearly all rainforest organisms are plagued by parasites and pathogens – organisms that feed on their hosts but give nothing in return.

society

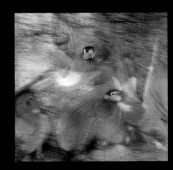

Most caterpillars lead furtive, solitary lives on the undersides of leaves, but those with stinging hairs and bright colours have little to fear from predators and occasionally mass together in conspicuous groups. Some form snake-like processions as they migrate from plant to plant, following the leader's scent trail in the search for fresh leaves. Others huddle together in a seething mass that emphasizes their warning colours, reinforcing the danger signal. Although adult butterflies are not really social creatures, in rainforests they are often seen crowded together in strange places, such as puddles of urine and mounds of animal droppings, and around corpses. The attraction is salt, protein, or other compounds that are lacking in the butterflies' diet of nectar.

◁ Stinging flag moth caterpillars
(Arctiidae) swarm up a tree trunk
in Manú National Park, Peru.

A group of around 30 saturniid caterpillars (Saturniidae) mass together to feed on shrubs in Manú National Park, Peru.

During a hike up the Alas River in Sumatra I stopped on the river bank to answer a call of nature. When I came back later the area was crowded with butterflies sucking urine from the sand. Rainforest butterflies often do this. Nectar contains very little but sugar and water and can only keep a butterfly going for a few weeks, but many tropical butterflies live longer than that and need dietary supplements, such as salt. To get minerals, butterflies suck moisture through their proboscis, extract the required salts, and squirt droplets of water from the anus every few seconds. Frequently the males collect salt and donate it to females in their sperm, which furnishes the females with the nutrients needed for the production of eggs. The butterflies' hunger for salt is so intense that you can quite easily catch one by offering a bead of sweat on the tip of your finger – it's my favourite trick for taking photographs of them.

▷ Drawn by the scent of urine, whites and sulphurs (Pieridae) congregate on the bank of Alas River in Gunung Leuser National Park, Sumatra, Indonesia.

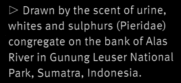

▷ Silverspot butterfly (*Dione moneta butleri*), Chiripo National Park, Costa Rica. ▽ Pierid butterflies (Pieridae), Gunung Leuser, Sumatra, Indonesia.

Pierid butterflies (Pieridae) alight collectively to gather minerals from a patch of damp ground at Iguaçu National Park, Brazil.

Butterflies are not the only animals that flock to
unusual locations in search of essential dietary
supplements. In the Amazon, macaws descend
screeching by the hundred onto crumbling
riverside cliffs. They come to swallow clay, the
minerals of which are thought to be an antidote
to poisons in seeds and nuts. Like most parrots,
macaws are highly sociable and garrulous.
While they feed they squawk noisily, but when
danger threatens they fall silent and still, before
taking to the air in an explosion of colour.

Clockwise from left to right: Red and Green
Macaws (*Ara chloroptera*), Rio Madre de
Dios, Peru; Scarlet Macaw (*Ara macao*),
Tambopata Reserve, Peru; Red and Green
Macaw, Rio Madre de Dios, Peru; Red and
Green Macaws, Rio Madre de Dios, Peru.

△ Orange-cheeked parrots
(*Pionopsitta barrabandi*),
and blue-headed parrots
(*Pionus menstruus*).
Tambopata Reserve, Peru.

◁ Visits to clay sites are
social occasions for mealy
parrots (*Amazona farinosa*).
Among the noisiest of parrots,
mealies maintain contact with
the flock with a complex range
of clucks, whistles, squawks,
and ear-splitting shrieks.
Tambopata Reserve, Peru.

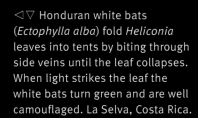

◁ ▽ Honduran white bats
(*Ectophylla alba*) fold *Heliconia*
leaves into tents by biting through
side veins until the leaf collapses.
When light strikes the leaf the
white bats turn green and are well
camouflaged. La Selva, Costa Rica.

While flocks of parrots cruise the rainforest for
food during the day, bats take over at night. The
focal point of bat social life is the communal
roost, where bats can spend more than half their
lives clustered together for safety and protection
from the elements. Caves and hollow trees make
the most secure roosting sites but rainforest bats
have found ingenious alternatives, including
hollow bamboo stems, tents constructed from
leaves, and giant cobwebs. Fruit bats simply
hang from the tree tops in colonies, or "camps",
that can contain as many as 8 million bats. They
frequently feed as a group, and travel long
distances in their search for food.

the easier it is to monopolize a tree and drive away rivals. Although primates can co-operate when they need to, life in the group is rarely harmonious. Primates, like humans, are competitive, and those that succeed get the choicest pickings. Climbing the social ladder, however, requires more than aggression — individuals must forge alliances, and keep a watchful eye on the relationships of others.

▷ A male black macaque stands apart from his troop. Unlike females, male black macaques are born outside the group, and must battle for dominance and privilege. Tangkoko Nature Reserve, Sulawesi, Indonesia.

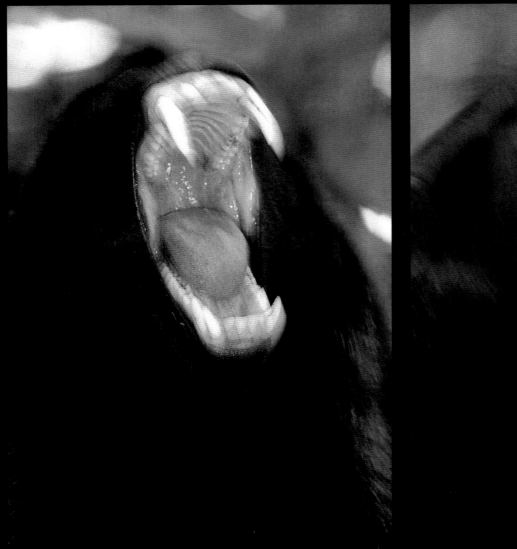

△▷ Like all monkeys, crested black macaques (*Macaca nigra*) communicate through sound, gesture, and the universal language of grooming. Between males, a yawn is an assertion of dominance, as it reveals the canine teeth. The larger the teeth, the higher the male is likely to be in the social group. Tangkoko Nature Reserve, Sulawesi, Indonesia.

Social arrangements vary hugely between primates and are closely related to diet. Fruit-eating monkeys live in large troops in which competition for food is fierce; as a consequence, their societies are aggressive and strongly hierarchical. Leaf-eaters such as colobus and proboscis monkeys, seem peaceful and egalitarian by comparison — their abundant food supplies mean that conflicts are infrequent. Gibbons and other apes subsist largely on fruit but can only digest the ripest. They have to spread out to find it, so their social groups tend to be small or widely dispersed. Marmosets and tamarins vary their diet of fruit and insects with the gum from trees. They form tight-knit extended family groups with a vigorously defended forest territory. When rival families meet, they screech angrily, fluff up their manes and whiskers, and leap at each other, biting.

◁ A single pair of breeding adults rules the social groups of common marmosets (*Callithrix jacchus*). Oddly, these tiny monkeys nearly always give birth to twins. Rio de Janeiro, Brazil.

△ Golden lion tamarin (*Leontopithecus rosalia*),
Poço das Antas Reserve, Brazil.

△ Black and white colobus monkey (*Colobus guereza*),
Mount Kenya National Park, Kenya.

△ Black and white ruffed lemur (*Varecia variegata variegata*), Toamasina, Madagascar.

△ Long-tailed macaque (*Macaca fascicularis*), Bako National Park, Borneo.

△ Proboscis monkey (*Nasalis larvatus*), Bako National Park, Borneo.

△ Wooley monkey (*Lagothrix*), Colombia.

A pair of squirrel monkeys (*Saimiri sciureus*) in Amacayacu National Park, Colombia. These highly sociable monkeys form groups of up to 200 members, or more.

Most social primates live in well defined groups, but chimpanzee society is more complex and in some respects more like our own. Common chimpanzees live in communities of up to 150 members but are seldom together. They spend most of their time foraging in small groups or alone and may not see each other for weeks, especially in the dry season when food is thinly scattered. Yet when they do meet, they remember each other and relationships are maintained. Their social world is violent, promiscuous, and political. Males wage frequent battles for dominance and form shifting coalitions with each other on their way to the top. Females are more solitary and less powerful but can use sex to gain influence. They mate with all the males, in exchange for food and protection, but reserve their most fertile period for the alpha male. In contrast, the bonobos of the Congo basin live in less seasonal rainforest and so have less need to disperse in search of food. Their society is tighter, with the females forming alliances that establish supremacy over males. And while grooming is the glue that binds common chimpanzee societies together, bonobos use ritualized sex to greet each other, celebrate, and resolve conflicts within the group.

▽▷ Chimpanzees communicate over distance with "pant hoots" – a crescendo of hoots building to a deafening screech. Such calls draw the dispersed members of a group together at trees in fruit. Kibale National Park, Uganda.

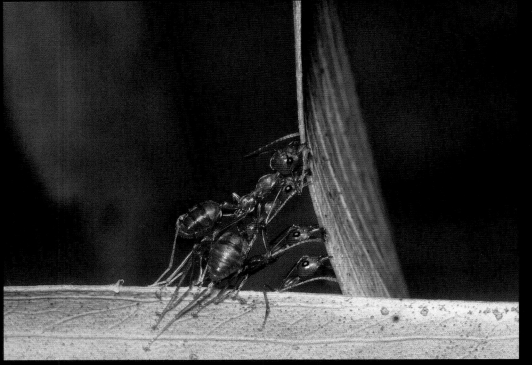

Insects have a more regimented social structure then primates, with individuals having specific tasks. Social insects, such as termites and ants, live everywhere in rainforests. They form colonies of varying sizes, some containing just a few individuals, while others number millions. The ants of every colony are classified by caste, and each caste is allocated a job within the colony, dependent upon it ability to reproduce. Ants that build permanent nests in trees have a symbiotic relationship with their host. The tree provides shelter and nectar from special glands on leaves, and the ants rid the tree of pests.

◁▽ Green tree ants (*Oecophylla smaragdina*) build nests from living leaves. The workers position the leaves, and bind them with silk squirted out of their larvae. Kakadu National Park, Australia.

△ Their bodies linked to form
a bridge, forest ants (Formicidae)
create a shortcut to the nest for
other members of their colony. Doi
Inthanon National Park, Thailand

Tree-dwelling ants do not always protect their host plants assiduously. Some insect pests bribe their way past the ants by secreting sugary fluids that are tastier than the tree's nectar. Tempted by this superior offering, the ants switch allegiance and guard the pests instead, allowing them to feed with impunity and protecting them from parasitic wasps. Lycaenid caterpillars are especially good at exploiting ants this way and sometimes go even further, producing pheromones that mimic ant larvae. Fooled into thinking the caterpillar is a giant ant grub, the ants carry it deep into their nest and place it among their larvae, which the caterpillar then begins to devour.

◁ Ants stand guard around a lycaenid caterpillar (Lycaenidae), which has tricked its way into their nest. Koh Samui, Thailand.

△ Caught on a long-exposure photograph, this colony of bees looks like a swarm of streaks. Manú National Park, Peru.

While ants mostly live in large, and always well-organized societies, bees and wasps have social arrangements that vary from solitary living to enormous, communal nests. Social wasps build their nests from mud or chewed-up plant fibres. The simplest of these consist of a few hexagonal chambers suspended from a leaf; more elaborate constructions have several storeys, outer walls, and entrance holes. The wasps stock the chambers with paralyzed insects and the queen lays eggs in them. Bees also build a honeycomb of chambers, but since they are for storing honey as well as grubs, the combs are hung vertically. The conventional wisdom that bees and wasps do not attack until provoked is not always true in rainforests. Some species will attack any passing animal, pursuing it for hundreds of metres.

△ Wasps start work on a paper nest suspended from a *Heliconia* leaf. Manú National Park, Peru.

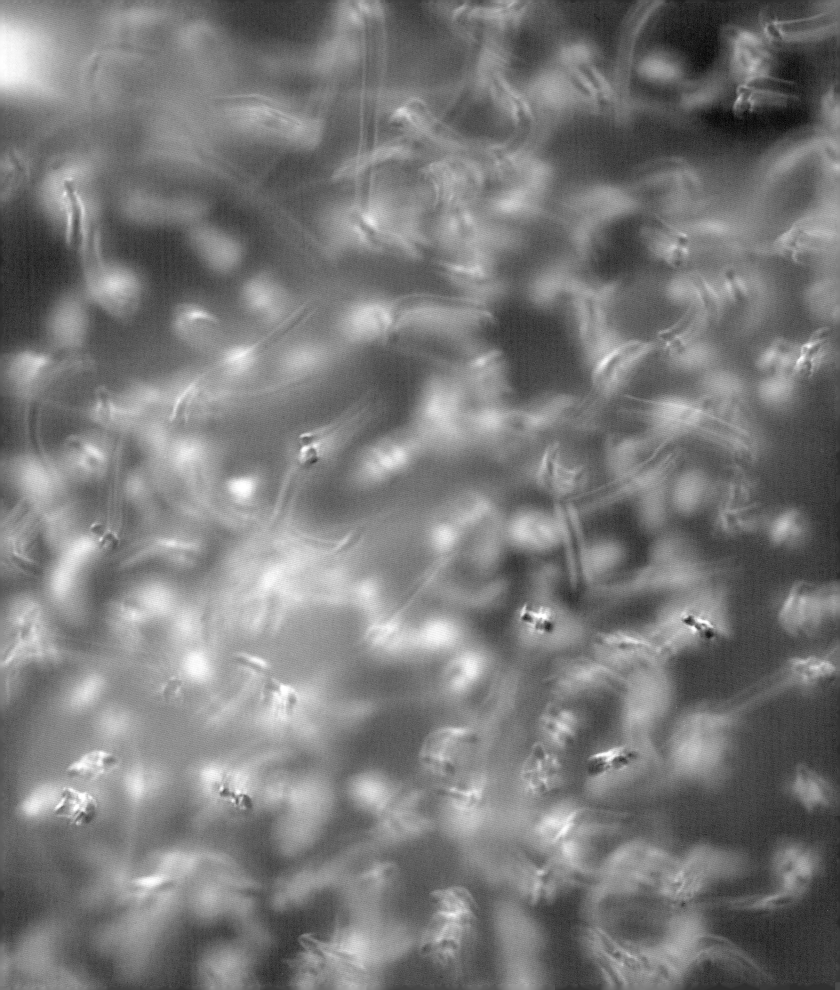

◁ Its dagger-like proboscis drawn, a horsefly prepares to impale a green treesnake (*Philodryas viridissimus*). As with mosquitos, only the females are bloodsuckers. Manú National Park, Peru.

Close relationships between animals do not always work to their mutual advantage, as each partner works purely out of self interest. Pests and parasites survive by theft or exploitation, and nothing in a rainforest can escape them. Some land briefly on victims to suck blood or implant flesh-eating larvae. Others fasten themselves to hair and skin, worm their way into intestines, wriggle into eyes, or insidiously burrow deep into muscle. The pests are themselves infested with pests of their own, many of which are more deadly: mosquitos carry the microbes that cause malaria, yellow fever, and dengue fever; sandflies inject germs that can eat away a person's face. Every animal in a rainforest is a walking zoo, infested by legions of miniature enemies, from viruses and bacteria to leeches and lice.

△ Not even this tiny green treefrog (*Litoria gracilenta*) can detect the light feet of a mosquito. Mossman Gorge, Australia.

▷▷ Male millipedes court females by walking along their backs, stimulating them with rhythmic pulses. Millipedes (Diplopoda), Mombasa, Kenya.

343

SOCIETY

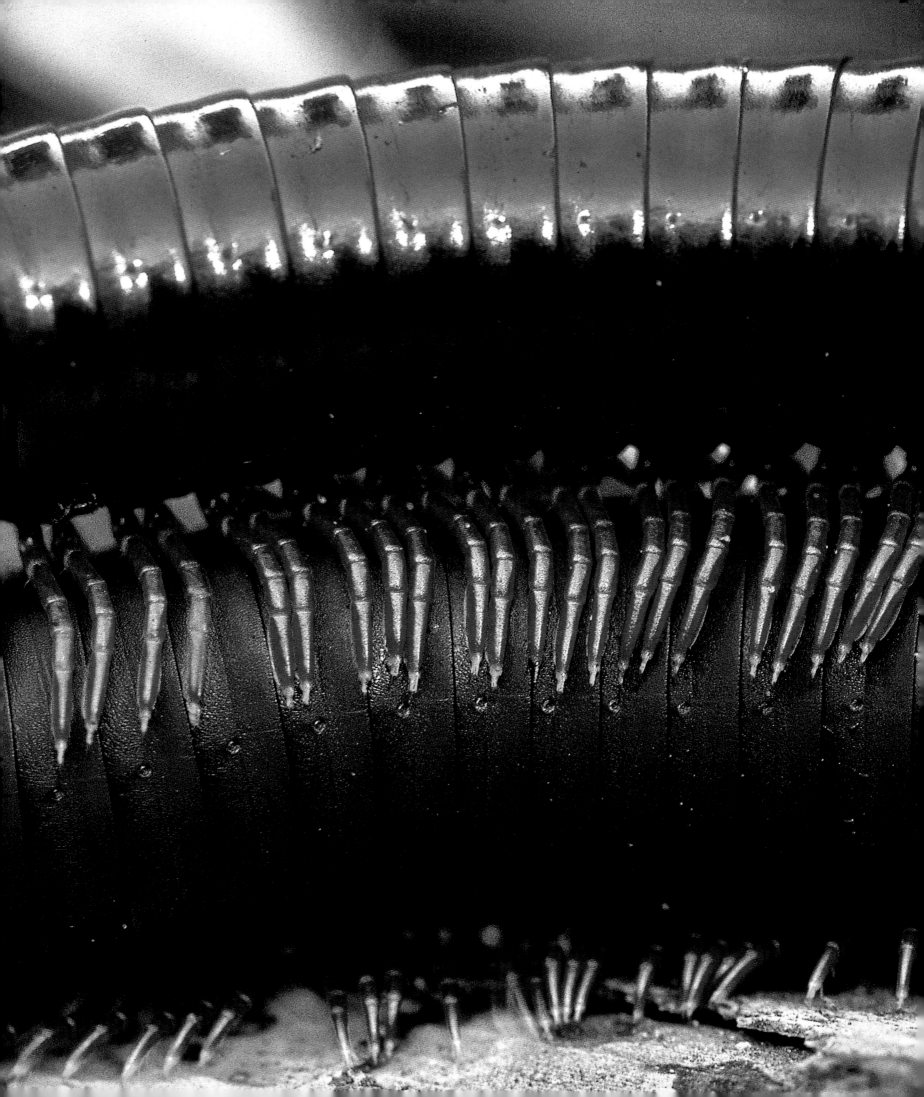

rainforests of the world

Rainforests cover six per cent of the Earth's land surface. They are at their most spectacular in tropical regions, but some types of rainforest extend as far north as Canada and as far south as Chile.

The world's largest remaining swathe of rainforest is found in the Amazon River basin in South America. Over half of this rainforest lies in Brazil, which holds about one-third of the world's remaining tropical rainforests. Another 20 per cent is found in Indonesia in Southeast Asia and the Congo River Basin in Central Africa, while the balance is scattered around the globe in tropical regions. The locations of rainforests are governed by global rainfall patterns. In general, the heaviest rainfalls are found in the tropics – the regions that receive the most sunlight throughout the year, between the tropics of Cancer and Capricorn. The strong heating system around the tropics creates wind systems that carry moisture off the sea and onto the land, creating hot, humid lowland regions – the typical tropical rainforests. At higher altitudes, conditions may be cooler but also wetter, giving rise to cloud forests in isolated highland areas. To the north and south of the tropics, some temperate coasts also receive enough moisture from rain and fog to host their own rainforests.

NORTH AND CENTRAL AMERICA

SOUTH AMERICA

wealth of the rainforests

- One-fifth of the world's fresh water is in the Amazon River Basin.
- Almost half the medicines we use every day come from plants endemic to the rainforest.
- A single pond in Brazil can sustain a greater variety of fish than is found in all of Europe's rivers.
- If present rates of destruction continue, there will be no rainforests remaining by 2060.

TROPICAL RAINFOREST

Lowland tropical rainforest is the most dense and verdant type and most closely resembles the classic image of a "jungle". It is hot, sticky and humid, and occurs at low altitudes, in river basins and along coasts. The tallest trees grow to great heights before branching, forming a high canopy with an open region beneath for a lower understorey. The tallest trees, called emergents, often grow several metres above the canopy.

CLOUD FOREST

These forests always occur at higher altitudes than lowland tropical rainforests. In some places they blend seamlessly with the lowland forests, but where lowland conditions are too arid, but there is more rain in the hills and mountains, they can rise above lowland plains and savannah grasslands. The trees in cloud forests tend to be shorter and hardier, since they have to endure thinner air and a wider range of temperatures. There are also more epiphytes – plants that live on the trunks and branches of other plants, such as mosses, ferns, orchids and bromeliads.

EUROPE

ASIA

RAINFOREST KEY		TROPICAL RAINFOREST
CLOUD FOREST		TEMPERATE RAINFOREST

TROPIC OF CANCER

AFRICA

EQUATOR

TROPIC OF CAPRICORN

AUSTRALASIA

TEMPERATE RAINFOREST

These forests often have coniferous trees alongside or replacing broadleaf species. They are often found in coastal areas, where the plants can absorb moisture from lingering sea fogs as well as rainfall. Coniferous rainforest trees can be extremely long-lived – often up to several hundred years, and may tower for tens of metres into the air before branching (one example is the giant redwood of North America's Pacific coast).

north and central america

Much of Central America is covered in tropical rainforest, while the Pacific coast of North America hosts a huge temperate forest.

The narrow neck of land that joins North and South America is sandwiched between the Atlantic and Pacific weather systems, and lies directly in the path of the trade winds blowing across the Atlantic from the northeast. As a result, Central America receives some of the heaviest rainfalls in the world. It also lies just north of the equator, meaning it experiences hot weather all the year round. The dense forests of the Chocó-Darién region are evidence of the fertile conditions in this part of the world, but rainforests run all the way along the Central American isthmus to Mexico, and are also found on many Caribbean islands. In North America, the coastline of the Pacific northwest experiences moisture-laden fog and heavy rainfall off the Pacific Ocean through much of the year. These damp conditions support the largest continuous area of coastal temperate rainforest in the world, which extends from Alaska to Oregon. North America's coastal rainforests contain at least 350 species of birds and animals and 25 tree species, many of which grow to an immense size and live very long lives.

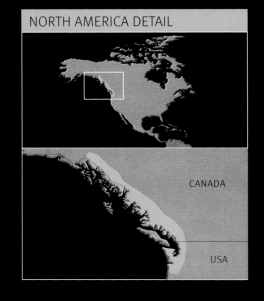

NORTH AMERICA DETAIL

CANADA

USA

MEXICO

1 TALAMANCAN CLOUD FORESTS

LOCATION Along the central mountain ranges of Costa Rica and western Panama.

TOTAL AREA 16,300 square kilometres.

KEY SPECIES Harpy eagle, resplendent quetzal, around 300 orchid species, 175 species of fern, numerous endemic birds and rare butterflies.

The central location of these cloud forests on the "land bridge" between North and South America has encouraged the mix of species from both continents and the rise of endemic species. The climate in this region is variable, due to the exposure it receives from both Pacific and Atlantic weather systems. Steep-sided mountains create a forest with conditions suitable for a huge variety of plant and animal species, making this one of the most diverse rainforests on the planet.

Strawberry poison frog (*Dendrobates pumilio*), Braulio Carillo National Park, Costa Rica.

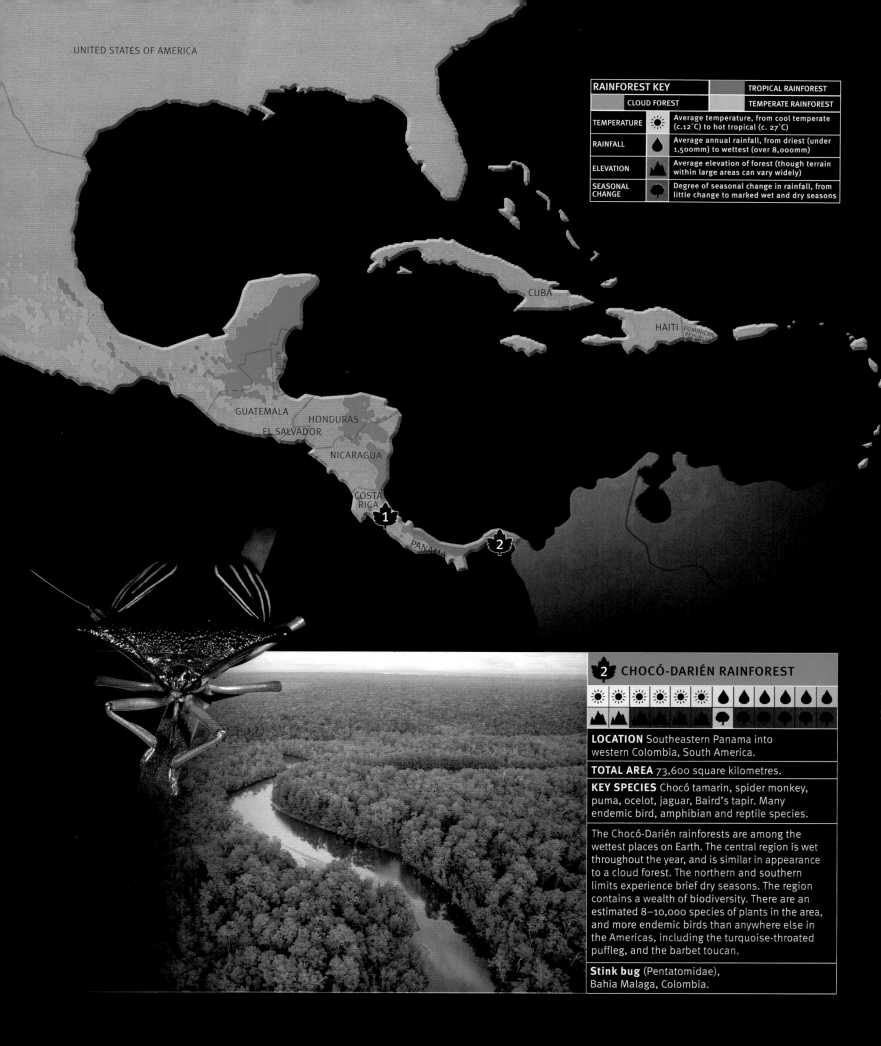

UNITED STATES OF AMERICA

CUBA

HAITI DOMINICAN REPUBLIC

BELIZE

GUATEMALA   HONDURAS
EL SALVADOR

NICARAGUA

COSTA
RICA

1

2

PANAMA

RAINFOREST KEY

RAINFOREST KEY	TROPICAL RAINFOREST
CLOUD FOREST	TEMPERATE RAINFOREST

TEMPERATURE	☀	Average temperature, from cool temperate (c.12°C) to hot tropical (c. 27°C)
RAINFALL	💧	Average annual rainfall, from driest (under 1,500mm) to wettest (over 8,000mm)
ELEVATION	⛰	Average elevation of forest (though terrain within large areas can vary widely)
SEASONAL CHANGE	🌳	Degree of seasonal change in rainfall, from little change to marked wet and dry seasons

2 CHOCÓ-DARIÉN RAINFOREST

LOCATION Southeastern Panama into western Colombia, South America.

TOTAL AREA 73,600 square kilometres.

KEY SPECIES Chocó tamarin, spider monkey, puma, ocelot, jaguar, Baird's tapir. Many endemic bird, amphibian and reptile species.

The Chocó-Darién rainforests are among the wettest places on Earth. The central region is wet throughout the year, and is similar in appearance to a cloud forest. The northern and southern limits experience brief dry seasons. The region contains a wealth of biodiversity. There are an estimated 8–10,000 species of plants in the area, and more endemic birds than anywhere else in the Americas, including the turquoise-throated puffleg, and the barbet toucan.

Stink bug (Pentatomidae), Bahia Malaga, Colombia.

south america

South America's rainforests extend from the tropics of Amazonia to the western slopes of the Andes in Chile.

The Andes mountains run like a spine close to South America's west coast, and have a profound effect on the continent's climate. They form a barrier that causes most of the continent's rainfall to drain eastwards into the South Atlantic Ocean, through a web of tributaries that lead into a handful of major rivers such as the Orinoco, Amazon, and Rio de la Plata. The South Atlantic itself forms a huge recycling system. In the tropical regions, water evaporates from the warm surface of the ocean, and is carried back onto the South American continent by the prevailing northwesterly trade winds. As a result, South America's rainforests are most dense in the tropical regions.

The Amazon rainforest is approximately the size of the 48 contiguous United States and is the largest rainforest on Earth. Its biodiversity is astonishing – perhaps 30 per cent of the world's species are found there. Around its edges, cloud forests rise from the low landscape into the foothills of the Andes to the west, and onto the Guyana plateau to the north. There are also patches of subtropical rainforest as far as the northern tip of Argentina. Further south, the cold, moist conditions of the Pacific coast create fogs and heavy rainfall that sustain a lengthy strip of temperate rainforest running through much of southern Chile.

![leaf] 1 GUIANA HIGHLANDS CLOUD FORESTS

LOCATION Northern Brazil, southern Venezuela, eastern Colombia, western Guyana.

TOTAL AREA 337,600 square kilometres.

KEY SPECIES Many typical Amazonian species including puma, jaguar, tapir, peccary, deer, boa constrictor, iguanas, hummingbirds.

The northern reaches of the Amazon Basin lie on the Guyana Shield, a raised rock plateau that isolates a region of quite seasonal and humid cloud forest from its lowland surroundings. The result is a region of enormous trees and a dense canopy, scattered across the plateau's plains and lower hills. In the midst of this rise huge, flat-topped, sheer-walled towers called Tepuis. The region is high in biodiversity, with many endemic plant, bat, bird, and reptile species.

Black and yellow poison frog (*Dendrobates leucomelas*), Canaima National Park, Venezuela.

2 AMAZON RAINFOREST

LOCATION Brazil, Peru, and Bolivia, stretching into neighbouring countries.

TOTAL AREA 6 million square kilometres.

KEY SPECIES Mammals, such as jaguar, giant otter, two-toed sloth, primates; countless bird and reptile species; about 18,000 plant species.

The rainforests that surround the River Amazon and its tributaries are a mosaic of ecosystems and vegetation types. The rainforest is typically made up of a canopy 30–40m high, with occasional emergent trees breaking through to reach 50m. Some regions experience annual floods that turn whole areas of the forest into a vast lake. The Amazon rainforest is one of the most ecologically diverse and rich areas of the planet; one hectare alone holds more than 246 species of trees.

Gesneriad flower,
Manú National Park, Peru.

RAINFOREST KEY		TROPICAL RAINFOREST
	CLOUD FOREST	TEMPERATE RAINFOREST
TEMPERATURE		Average temperature, from cool temperate (c.12˚C) to hot tropical (c.27˚C)
RAINFALL		Average annual rainfall, from driest (under 1,500mm) to wettest (over 8,000mm)
ELEVATION		Average elevation of forest (though terrain within large areas can vary widely)
SEASONAL CHANGE		Degree of seasonal change in rainfall, from little change to marked wet and dry seasons

3 ALTA PARANÁ RAINFORESTS

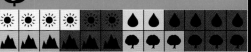

LOCATION Southern Brazil, eastern Paraguay and northeastern Argentina.

TOTAL AREA 483,800 square kilometres.

KEY SPECIES Gold-rumped lion tamarin, brown howler monkey, ocelot, helmeted woodcreeper, São Paolo tyrannulet.

The Alta Paraná forests are subtropical – that is, they lie south of the tropics, in a region that experiences a pronounced dry season with regular frosts from April to September. They rise from the river plains up to the Brazilian plateau at an elevation of 800m, and are broken into scattered fragments, with a few larger blocks such as the Brazilian and Argentinian national parks surrounding the spectacular Iguaçu Falls on the border between the two countries.

Plovercrest hummingbird (*Stephanoxis lalandi*),
Iguaçu National Park, Brazil.

africa

Africa contains the second largest rainforest in the world, in a broad band centred on the equator.

The most significant concentration of tropical rainforest in Africa lies around the Congo River Basin. Its equatorial position means the Congo is hot and humid all year round, receiving most of its rainfall from moisture-laden air carried onto the continent from the South Atlantic. Similar factors create a long, patchy strip of rainforest along the south coast of West Africa. The African rainforest was once much larger – it has retreated in the 10,000 years since the end of the last Ice Age, as deserts have expanded from the north and savannah grasslands have spread from the east. A few isolated fragments of the ancient forest still survive where conditions support them, such as in the highland regions of Tanzania and Kenya in East Africa. Another patchy region of forest is found in and around Mozambique. The constant rainfall received along the east coast of Madagascar, the world's fourth largest island, fosters tropical rainforests that are home to some 250,000 species, 70 per cent of which are found nowhere else on the planet.

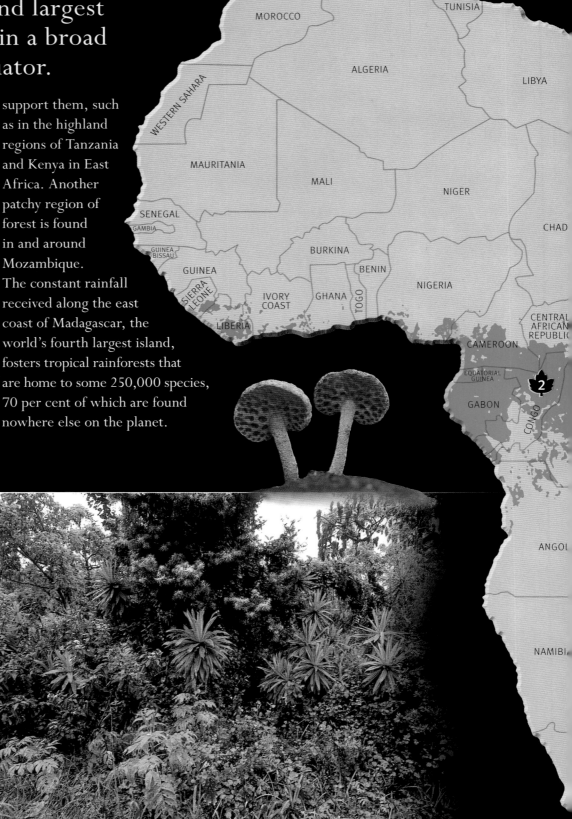

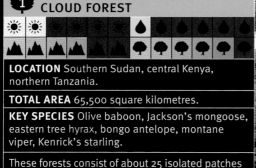

EAST AFRICAN HIGHLAND CLOUD FOREST

LOCATION Southern Sudan, central Kenya, northern Tanzania.

TOTAL AREA 65,500 square kilometres.

KEY SPECIES Olive baboon, Jackson's mongoose, eastern tree hyrax, bongo antelope, montane viper, Kenrick's starling.

These forests consist of about 25 isolated patches on either side of the equator. They include the slopes of Mount Kenya, Mount Kilimanjaro, and the western side of the Great Rift Valley. Despite the heat on the plains below, above 1,000m the conditions are wet enough for cloud forests to thrive. A number of mammal and reptile species (especially chameleons) are unique to the habitat, but others, like the bongo antelope, seem to have been stranded by the retreating Congo rainforests.

Mushrooms (*Favolaschia*), Mount Kenya National Park, Kenya.

2 CONGO RAINFOREST

| ☀ | ☀ | ☀ | ☀ | ☀ | | 💧 | 💧 | | ♠ | ♠ | ♠ |
| ⛰ | | | | | | 🍀 | 🍀 | | ♠ | ♠ | ♠ |

LOCATION A huge region of central Africa centred around the Democratic Republic of Congo.

TOTAL AREA 1.9 million square kilometres.

KEY SPECIES Forest elephant, chimpanzees, bonobo, DeBrazza's monkey, okapi, bongo antelope, lowland and mountain gorilla.

The Congo is one of the least explored rainforests on Earth, partly because it is difficult to access. It is divided into a number of distinct units, ranging from swamp forests in the Congo Basin to cloud forests located in the mountains of Rwanda. The heart of the forest is extremely wet and humid, with little seasonal variation. The Congo is home to around 11,000 plant species, including trees such as iroko, sapele, and mahogany, and 800 different mammal species.

Chimpanzee (*Pan troglodytes*), Western Congolian swamp forest, Congo.

RAINFOREST KEY			TROPICAL RAINFOREST
CLOUD FOREST			TEMPERATE RAINFOREST
TEMPERATURE	☀	Average temperature, from cool temperate (c.12˚C) to hot tropical (c. 27˚C)	
RAINFALL	💧	Average annual rainfall, from driest (under 1,500mm) to wettest (over 8,000mm)	
ELEVATION	⛰	Average elevation of forest (though terrain within large areas can vary widely)	
SEASONAL CHANGE	♣	Degree of seasonal change in rainfall, from little change to marked wet and dry seasons	

---

3 MADAGASCAR RAINFORESTS

| ☀ | ☀ | ☀ | ☀ | | 💧 | 💧 | 🔺 | 🔺 | 🔺 | 🔺 |
| ⛰ | ⛰ | ⛰ | ⛰ | | 🍀 | 🍀 | 🍀 | 🍀 | 🍀 | 🍀 |

LOCATION The island of Madagascar, concentrated along the east coast.

TOTAL AREA 38,000 square kilometres.

KEY SPECIES Fossa, Madagascar red owl, various lemurs, nocturnal aye-aye, Malagasy tomato frog. Huge variety of chameleons and insects.

Madagascar's rainforests are one of the world's most unique environments – a haven where life has evolved along a different path since the island separated from mainland Africa and India tens of millions of years ago. The numerous different rainforest habitats are home to many of Madagascar's notable animals, including the unique lemurs and many different species of chameleons. New plants and animals are still regularly discovered in Madagascar's rainforests.

Parson's chameleon (*Calumma parsonii cristifer*), Mantadia National Park, Madagascar.

asia

Asia's lush rainforests hug the coast of the mainland and range across the continent's numerous tropical islands.

Although the dry interior of the Asian continent is unable to sustain rainforests, some areas around the edge receive heavy annual rainfall, and these have given rise to dense and diverse rainforests. The largest swathes are found in the southwest and southeast of the continent, scattered across the tropical islands of Indonesia, on the Malay Peninsula (Malaysia, Thailand and Myanmar) and in Laos, Vietnam and Cambodia. There are also patches of rainforest on the wetter, western half of the Indian peninsular and on the west coast of Sri Lanka. Bangladesh has the largest area of mangrove forests in the world. Southeast Asia is one of the world's most biologically diverse regions – the island of Borneo alone has between 10,000 and 15,000 species of flowering plant. Indonesia is particularly rich in biodiversity, with 16 per cent of the world's bird species, 11 per cent of its plants, including the Rafflesia, the world's largest flower, and 10 per cent of its mammals, including the orang-utan and the Sumatran tiger, neither of which is found elsewhere. Indonesia's rainforests are also some of the oldest on Earth – scientists believe they may have existed for more than 100 million years, though only fragments of the original forest remain and the rate of loss is very high.

1 BORNEO CLOUD FORESTS

LOCATION The island of Borneo – the countries of Indonesia, Malaysia, and Brunei.

TOTAL AREA 115,600 square kilometres.

KEY SPECIES Orang-utans, gibbons, langurs, macaques, Sumatran rhino, pitcher plants, mountain serpent-eagle, black oriole.

The highland cloud forests of Borneo are islands in a sea of lowland rainforests. Developing in isolation, they have given rise to many unique species. The lower reaches of the Bornean highlands are covered by forests dominated by the local species of oak and chestnut, but above 1,500m, shrubby "ericaceous" plants, tolerant of acid soils, become dominant. Borneo's forests are home to about 150 mammal species, and some 250 species of bird.

BLUE PANSY (*Junonia orythia*), Gunung Mulu National Park, Sarawak, Malaysia.

CHINA

MYANMAR

LAOS

THAILAND

CAMBODIA

VIETNAM

PHILIPPINES

PHILIPPINES

BRUNEI

MALAYSIA

MALAYSIA

BORNEO

SUMATRA

INDONESIA

INDONESIA

SULAWESI

INDONESIA

NEW GUINEA

JAVA

1

2

RAINFOREST KEY		TROPICAL RAINFOREST
	CLOUD FOREST	TEMPERATE RAINFOREST
TEMPERATURE	☀	Average temperature, from cool temperate (c.12˚C) to hot tropical (c. 27˚C)
RAINFALL	💧	Average annual rainfall, from driest (under 1,500mm) to wettest (over 8,000mm)
ELEVATION	⛰	Average elevation of forest (though terrain within large areas can vary widely)
SEASONAL CHANGE	🌳	Degree of seasonal change in rainfall, from little change to marked wet and dry seasons

2 SUMATRAN RAINFOREST

LOCATION
The island of Sumatra in Indonesia.

TOTAL AREA 332,400 square kilometres.

KEY SPECIES Sumatran rabbit, Thomas's leaf monkey, orang-utans, Sumatran tiger, Sumatran rhino, sun bear, Rafflesia plants.

Much of Sumatra is covered in dense rainforest. Tropical forests cover many lowland areas, while cloud forests run along the Barisan mountain range on the western side of the island. The lowland forests are dominated by flowering dipterocarp trees that create a dense canopy. At higher elevations, these are mixed with oaks and laurels, among other tree species. Further up, these blend into relatively low coniferous plants such as rhododendron and eucalyptus.

Cicada (Cicadidae), Gunung Leuser National Park, Indonesia.

australasia

The rainforests of Australasia range from lush New Guinea jungles, through ancient Queensland forests, to cold New Zealand woodlands.

Australasia is affected by a number of different weather systems, which give rise to a huge variety of climates, including some regions suitable for flourishing rainforests. New Guinea marks the boundary between Australasia and Southeast Asia, and experiences the same year-round warm, wet weather conditions. Its rainforests are densely packed with trees and shrubs. Australia itself sits in the tropical regions of the southern hemisphere, and much of the continent's vast interior is arid and desert-like. The exception is the east coast of the country, which lies in the path of moisture-laden trade winds blowing across the South Pacific from the southeast. As a result, the coast of northeastern Australia is host to a strip of ancient rainforest – probably the oldest forest in continuous existence anywhere on the planet – a remnant from the great forests of a long-vanished supercontinent. Isolated in the South Pacific and somewhat further to the south, New Zealand offers a distinct contrast to the rest of Australasia. It is exposed to heavy rainfall and fogs brought by colder trade winds from the southeast. Its lush temperate rainforests are found in the southerly mountainous regions, and are notable for their high level of endemic plant-life.

AUSTRALIA

1 NEW GUINEA CLOUD FOREST

LOCATION Across the island of New Guinea, in Indonesia and Papua New Guinea.

TOTAL AREA 172,000 square kilometres.

KEY SPECIES Papuan forest wallaby, tree kangaroo, and other marsupials. Papuan swiftlet, several birds of paradise.

The island of New Guinea has a diverse mix of flora and fauna with both Asian and Australasian origins. Some of the cloud forests that run along the island's central mountain range have been isolated for thousands of years, and as a result many new species have evolved. Some plants are restricted to a single mountain peak. The lower forests contain oaks, laurels, and elaeocarp trees. Around 2,000 metres, these merge with moist forests overgrown with mosses.

Birdwing butterfly (*Ornithoptera priamus*), Crater Mountain National Park, Papua New Guinea.

2 NORTHEAST AUSTRALIAN RAINFORESTS

LOCATION Along Australia's northeast coast, particularly in southeast Queensland.

TOTAL AREA 32,700 square kilometres.

KEY SPECIES Mahogany glider, southern cassowary, armoured frog, tree kangaroo, golden bowerbird, Boyd's forest dragon.

This rainforest rises from lowlands near the coast to an inland plateau. Its most interesting aspect is its history – this small strip of forest is the direct descendant of the great rainforests of Gondwana, a supercontinent formed from Australasia, Africa, and South America which broke up around 200 million years ago. The great age of the forest is shown by the abundance of species that are sole survivors from families of plants that have long since died out elsewhere.

Praying mantis (Mantidae), Palmerston National Park, Queensland, Australia.

NEW ZEALAND DETAIL

RAINFOREST KEY

RAINFOREST KEY		TROPICAL RAINFOREST
	CLOUD FOREST	TEMPERATE RAINFOREST
TEMPERATURE		Average temperature, from cool temperate (c.12˚C) to hot tropical (c. 27˚C)
RAINFALL		Average annual rainfall, from driest (under 1,500mm) to wettest (over 8,000mm)
ELEVATION		Average elevation of forest (though terrain within large areas can vary widely)
SEASONAL CHANGE		Degree of seasonal change in rainfall, from little change to marked wet and dry seasons

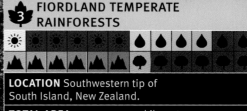

3 FIORDLAND TEMPERATE RAINFORESTS

LOCATION Southwestern tip of South Island, New Zealand.

TOTAL AREA 11,000 square kilometres.

KEY SPECIES Takahe parrot, kakapo (only surviving on offshore islands), Fiordland skink, many insect species.

The stunning landscape of southern New Zealand was shaped by glaciers during the last Ice Age, 10,000 years ago. Today, it is home to a temperate rainforest, descended from plants that survived the ice in sheltered areas. The forest is dominated by trees such as silver, red, and mountain beeches, reaching from the coast up to the tree line – many of the higher areas are covered with grassland and bogs. Almost the entire area is protected by the vast Fiordland National Park.

Pass Creek, Fiordland National Park, New Zealand.

PAPUA NEW GUINEA

NEW GUINEA

NEW ZEALAND

photographing the rainforest

Taking photographs in a rainforest is a painstaking process, and a game of chance and infinite patience. Investing time looking for the places where animals will come to eat or drink is usually my most useful strategy for capturing wildlife on film. Many of the creatures I've photographed were absorbed with feeding and often completely unaware or unconcerned by my presence. After a while I get to know about the behaviour of each animal I photograph, so I know how best to approach them and how I myself have to behave to get good shots. A big challenge for a wildlife photographer is finding the right lighting – I always aim to show the subject in natural lighting conditions, so I avoid using strong flashlights, except at night when there is no alternative. On the forest floor there is very little light, so to achieve sharp pictures I use long

exposure times, sometimes up to 30 seconds. Another challenge is looking after my gear in an environment where high levels of humidity, fast-changing weather conditions and condensation can cause havoc with even the most reliable equipment. I always work with Nikon cameras and lenses; I use their 17–35 mm wide-angle lenses a lot because with them I can show the subject within its natural environment. My favourite macro lens is the 200 mm, as I love to create a strong foreground interest to capture the viewer's attention. I can get through hundreds of films in the field – if I see a spectacular frog or butterfly I shoot at least one film of it (40 pictures). I change the angle, exposure, lens aperture, and so on, because I never know which picture is going to look best.

index

DK would like to thank the following people for their help in the preparation of this book: Dr Phillip Cribb at Royal Botanic Gardens, Kew. Professor Thomas Læssøe, Copenhagen University. Staff of the Herbarium and the Mycology Section, Royal Botanic Gardens, Kew. The team at MDP - Pete Draper, Mark Deamer, Dave Bennett, Nigel King, Jenney Deamer. (www.mdp-uk.com)

Thomas Marent would like to thank the following people for their help, support and encouragement: Manú Nature Tours, Peru; Steve Richards; Rainforest Expeditions, Peru; Associação Mico-Leão-Dourado; Ben Morgan; the creative team at DK London; Monika Schlitzer, at DK Germany.